HOUSEHOLD SALVATION

Colin Dye

Dovewell Publications

Dovewell Publications
PO Box 9161
London
W3 6GS
England

Copyright © 1998 by Colin Dye

All rights reserved. No part of this publication may be reproduced, stored in a retrieval system or transmitted, in any form or by any means, electronic, mechanical, photocopying or otherwise, without the prior written consent of the publisher.

Scriptural quotations are from the New King James Version, Thomas Nelson Inc., 1991.

ISBN 1 898 444 85 4

Designed and produced by Gazelle Creative Productions Ltd, Concorde House, Grenville Place, Mill Hill, London, NW7 3SA

CONTENTS

1. God's overflowing blessing — 5
2. God works in families — 12
3. God keeps His covenants — 19
4. God blesses a thousand generations — 25
5. God's covenant with Abram — 31
6. Family salvation — 38
7. New Covenant promises — 50
8. Strongholds come down — 61
9. Promises for your family — 68
10. Praying for your family — 78
11. Blessings and curses — 85
12. Freedom from curses — 99
13. Freedom for your family — 104
14. Can the devil curse you? — 110
15. Freedom from the past — 117
16. Honouring parents — 127
17. Parental blessing — 135
18. The family altar — 146

*Believe on the Lord Jesus Christ,
and you will be saved,
you and your household.*

Acts 16:31

1

God's overflowing blessing

Throughout history, some brilliant discoveries have been made which have shaped billions of lives.

Can you imagine how thrilling it must have been to discover fire, the wheel, bread, glass, cloth, the printing press, electricity, anaesthetics, antibiotics, the telephone, and so on?

Sometimes it seems as though there's nothing left for anyone to discover in the physical world. But I know that there are two fantastic discoveries which are just waiting for you to find in the spiritual world, in the person of Jesus Christ.

Your greatest discoveries

Dear friend, the two greatest discoveries that you can ever make are these:

⇒ *who you really are in Christ*

⇒ *what you genuinely have in Christ*

It may seem to you that these are not that world-shaking, that they don't really compare with finding a cure to cancer or a pollution-free source of power.

Yet, on the contrary, my friend, they're the most important pair of discoveries in the universe. When you recognise what God has revealed in Christ, you find lasting peace and wholeness, eternal hope and healing, infinite power and authority.

It's only when you finally grasp God's revelation of who you actually are *in Christ* – and what you truly have *in Him* – that you can enjoy the wonderful promises of overflowing blessing which accompany your eternal salvation.

These great promises have to do with living the abundant life which God has prepared for you. He wants *you* to discover a new, supernatural dimension of Christian living – and He longs for you to enter it fully, deeply, completely, right now!

Some people are against all talk of believers enjoying the blessing of God this side of heaven. They think that this is a selfish way to live.

The Bible, however, promises that we've already been blessed with every spiritual blessing in the heavenly realms in Christ Jesus.

Blessed be the God and Father of our Lord Jesus Christ, who has blessed us with every spiritual blessing in the heavenly places in Christ.

Ephesians 1:3

This verse doesn't look to the future. It doesn't promise that God *will* bless us in heaven (though He will). Instead, the verse looks to the past – it's a cast-iron guarantee that God *has* blessed us in Christ.

Because the Bible teaches, my friend, that God has blessed you with *every* spiritual blessing, don't you think that He wants you to experience and enjoy these blessings *now*, on earth, in the day-to-day life that you're living?

Of course He does! If *God* has given *you* every single spiritual blessing that there is in the heavenly places in Christ, He must surely want you to *enjoy* what He's given you.

But it doesn't stop here. God wants you to receive, to experience and to enjoy His blessings for a very important reason. He causes His blessings to cascade from Him to you so that they can overflow from you to the people around you.

You're blessed to bless others

That's what this book is about – you becoming an overflowing blessing to others, especially to your family.

Through this book, dear friend, I want to help you to start experiencing all the spiritual blessings that God has already given you.

But I don't want you to enjoy them selfishly, just for your own sake; I want you to experience God's blessings so that they can overflow from you to others – especially to the members of your family.

In this book, you'll discover that God has given some very precious and effective promises for the families, for the households, of believers.

And you'll learn how to lay hold of these wonderful promises – so that *your family* may find true freedom and begin to live in the goodness of God's abundant blessings.

Your faith can count for your family

Your personal faith in Christ can have a profound and far-reaching effect on the whole of your family – on your parents, your spouse, your brothers and sisters, your children and grandchildren, and so on.

In fact, as a believer, you hold the key to your family's well-being. And not just to your immediate family: your entire family bloodline can benefit from God's blessing because of your obedient faith in Christ.

Know that the Lord your God, He is God, the faithful God who keeps covenant and mercy for a thousand generations with those who love Him and keep His commandments. Deuteronomy 7:9

My dear friend, because you're a child of the covenant, God will bless those who are close to you. And, if they're willing, they can enter His fullness for themselves!

Your family can be set free

We can all think of certain family traits and characteristics which spoil the lives of some members of our families.

For example, there may be a history of miscarriages or bankruptcy in your family. Or there may be a long line of divorces among your relatives – both past and present.

Or you may be able to catalogue a series of accidents or tragedies which seem to recur in every generation of your family.

In this book, you'll discover how your faith can reverse the negative traits in your family which seem to have been passed down through the generations.

In Christ, God has provided you with the means to ensure that your whole family is set free from all these unpleasant, harmful things.

Your family can be saved

Household Salvation is one of the most important promises that God gives you. He guarantees to deal graciously with all the members of your family.

And, as soon as they're willing to let Him work in their lives, God will save them.

Believe on the Lord Jesus Christ, and you will be saved, you and your household.   Acts 16:31

For far too long, Christianity in Western Europe and North America has concentrated almost exclusively on the *individual* aspects of serving God and following Christ.

But the great truths of personal faith in Jesus, personal blessing from God and a personal relationship with the Spirit must not cause us to miss the *corporate* dimension of our faith.

Choose for yourselves this day whom you will serve.... But as for me and my house, we will serve the Lord. Joshua 24:15

This book will show you how God deals with whole families – with entire households – not just with individual men and women who believe.

And it will explain the biblical revelation that God purposes to bless complete families by setting them free to enjoy all the blessings of His covenant.

But first, my friend, you need to begin by understanding a very important biblical principle – that it really is God's plan to touch *your* whole family through *you*.

2

God works in families

When you first believed in Jesus as your Lord and Saviour, you entered into a *personal* relationship with God. He dealt with you as an *individual*, and His blessings began to flow into your life.

But, dear friend, you weren't saved by God to live His life of faith in splendid isolation. Instead, the Father adopted you into His redeemed family, and now you can never be alone.

God sets the solitary in families   Psalm 68:6

The church of Jesus Christ is a universal family which transcends heaven and earth. It's made of all the different brothers and sisters, from every age and continent, who know and love God. They live together – in heaven and on earth – in a glorious fellowship, in the community of saints.

This means, my friend, that – together in Christ with all the other believers who've ever lived – we're part of the same single *holy family*.

God's family image

Believers in western nations don't have a very clear picture of God's family. We're used to a more 'individualistic' way of thinking.

We tend to read the New Testament as though it were written to each of us individually, rather than to all of us *corporately*. We assume that the New Testament word 'you' means 'you on your own', when it nearly always means 'you all'.

And many of us think that we've been made individually in the image of an individual God. Yet the Bible shows that it was a triune God who made the whole of humanity in His corporate image.

God created mankind in His own image.... male and female He created them.   Genesis 1:27

This suggests that it's our corporate relationships – our loving inter-dependence with each other – which particularly reflects the family life of God.

Indeed, the New Testament makes it clear that every earthly family has its source in the divine life of the Father and the Son.

I bow my knees to the Father of our Lord Jesus Christ, from whom the whole family in heaven and earth is named.   Ephesians 3:15

Too many western believers consider themselves as separate individuals – like islands in a vast ocean. But God looks on us, and deals with us, quite differently.

He sees us not only as individuals, but also as families and groups of people. And God has a plan for our lives at every one of these levels.

As individuals, we have full responsibility for our personal actions. Each one of us must believe in Christ for ourselves. We must personally turn from our sins and embrace His grace.

In the Bible, however, we don't find God blessing only individual people. He also blesses families, households, tribes, villages, urban communities, even whole nations.

God weaves His plans and purposes far beyond individual lives – out into communities, and even across many generations of people.

The God of the generations

Many believers are pre-occupied with God's will for their personal lives. But you, dear friend, need to recognise that His plans for you extend beyond your individual life.

God's holy purposes for you are fully intertwined with His purposes for your family, your household, your community, your local church, your town, your nation – for all the people around you.

He's the God of history, and He's been at work through all generations.

To a large extent, you're who you are as a result of the way that your parents, grandparents and great-grandparents responded to God's love.

And your spouse, children, grandchildren and great-grandchildren will – in their turn – be shaped by the way that you respond to God's grace.

Quite simply, He's the God of Abraham, Isaac and Jacob. He's the God of the family generations.

When God revealed Himself to Abraham (he was called Abram at the time) God promised this:

I will bless you and make your name great; and you shall be a blessing.   Genesis 12:2

Abram's personal blessing hung on his response to God's call to leave Haran. But God chose to bless Abram so that he would be a blessing to others around him *and* to his descendants.

In fact, God's promise to Abram was:

In you all the families of the earth shall be blessed.   Genesis 12:3

God's purpose was to bring blessing to the whole world through Abram. No wonder God told him:

I will bless those who bless you, and I will curse him who curses you.   Genesis 12:3

We call this God's 'covenant' plan. This is a strange concept to some believers today, but the Bible shows that 'covenants' are at the heart of God's character – they're the way that He's always related to the people He's made.

God's covenant purpose has not changed. He still purposes to bless us so that, like Abram, we can be a blessing to others – including our descendants.

God's line of blessing

My dear friend, God wants you to live in the line of His blessing on earth. This is His way of ensuring that His blessings overflow from you to the people around you – so that they can enter God's fullness.

As well as coming to us directly in Christ, God's blessings also come to us down the generations from our parents, grandparents and ancestors.

I, the Lord your God, am a jealous God, visiting the iniquity of the fathers on the children to the third and fourth generations of those who hate Me, but showing mercy to thousands, to those who love Me and keep My commandments. Exodus 20:5-6

I'm sure you can see how this has affected you – how, in some way, you've been blessed because of your forefathers.

Pause now and list your 'generational blessings'. Then praise God for the way that He's blessed you through your family bloodline.

God's freedom from the line of judgement

As well as God's blessings flowing to you from past generations, God's righteous judgements on your forefathers can affect you in a negative way.

This is where you'll begin to see how the blood of Jesus truly sets you free!

Jesus Christ was Himself made a curse for you, and He took your judgement onto Himself. His shed blood has set you free from every bondage, every curse and every judgement of God.

This applies not only to the effects of your own sin on your life, but also to those negative effects which have been passed down to you through your bloodline from your sinful ancestors.

You were not redeemed with corruptible things, like silver or gold, from your aimless conduct received by tradition from your fathers, but with the precious blood of Christ, as of a lamb without blemish and without spot. 1 Peter 1:18-19

Later in this book, you'll learn how to make sure that you're experiencing and enjoying this amazing freedom. Before this, however, you must begin to understand more from the Bible about the 'New Covenant' that God's made with you.

3

God keeps His covenants

The Bible teaches that God is the God of covenant. This is how He deals with people today.

A covenant is simply a *binding agreement* between two different parties. In Bible days, many kinds of agreements were made between people, families, tribes and nations.

Most binding agreements were made between two equal parties. These sorts of promises or 'treaties' could be enforced quite easily, and were a sensible way of avoiding conflict.

A few binding agreements were made between a superior and an inferior person, or between a stronger and a weaker nation. In these cases, both parties promised to do or provide something of value for the other – and both agreed to be bound by the agreement.

Very occasionally, a powerful party promised to help a weaker party without expecting anything in return. These binding agreements guaranteed a great deal for the weaker party. They could promise peace, security, material provision, and so on.

In Old Testament times, the setting up of a binding agreement was a very solemn affair; and the most important were sealed by the sacrifice of valuable animals. These 'blood covenants' were especially binding upon the two parties.

God's blood covenant

All this is significant for you, dear friend, because, as a Christian believer, God has called you to live in a 'covenant' relationship with Himself.

God's binding agreement with you, His covenant, was sealed by the perfect, sacrificial blood of His only Son. This binds God in eternal faithfulness to keep all His promises to you. We call this *the New Covenant*, and it brings you into the fullness of God's richest blessing.

The New Covenant

As we've seen, the New Testament promises that we've been blessed with *every* spiritual blessing in heavenly places, in Christ Jesus. These blessings have come to us as part of God's New Covenant.

Even though we don't deserve these blessings, God's mercy and grace are poured into our lives, in Christ. This means that God's New Covenant blessings come to us entirely as a free gift of His own goodness. They have nothing to do with our own effort, works or goodness.

The Old Covenant

This is very different from *the Old Covenant* that God made with the people of Israel.

In Old Testament times, the blessing of God depended upon the people obeying the Law of Moses – whereas our blessing depends only on the righteousness and obedience of Christ.

Because of the New Covenant, we receive all the benefits of Jesus' sinless life as well as all the benefits of His sacrificial death.

This means, my friend, that, as a believer in Jesus, you're a prime candidate for His blessing!

Jesus has fulfilled every condition for your blessing, and now you're in the best possible place to experience all that God has for you. Hallelujah!

Although we live in New Covenant times, the Old Testament covenants still have much to teach us – for God's blessing and faithfulness were present in Old Testament times.

It's just that His New Covenant is much, much better the Old Covenant!

The New is more glorious than the Old

God's blessings have greatly *increased* in the New Covenant. His Old Covenant promises have not been overturned or reduced; instead, they've been incorporated into the New Covenant and have been raised to a far higher level in the Spirit.

Many people say that the Old Covenant brought only physical blessings while the New Covenant brings only spiritual blessings. This is *partly right*, but it's not the whole picture.

It's clear that God provided His Old Covenant people with many spiritual blessings. And it's crazy to suggest that God ignores the physical needs of His New Covenant people.

My dear friend, all the *essential* blessings of the Old Covenant belong to all God's people in every age. God still promises you healing, material provision, physical protection – and the other *key* blessings mentioned in the Old Testament.

Forgiveness of sins, peace with God, the abiding presence of the Spirit – and the other spiritual blessings described in the New Testament – have not replaced the Old Covenant blessings: they've simply been added to them.

All God's blessings come through the Spirit

The Holy Spirit has taken the essential Old Covenant physical blessings and lifted them to a much higher level. In-and-through the Spirit, they're no longer mere physical blessings – but they still do benefit us physically.

If you're to understand this correctly, you must realise that *all* God's blessings come to you in the Holy Spirit. It is He who is at work in you, shaping you, blessing you and making you like Jesus.

All the Old Covenant and New Covenant blessings of God flow from your Spirit-inspired,

Spirit-directed and Spirit-enabled relationship with Jesus Christ.

In fact, every single blessing is based *in the Holy Spirit* – who is Himself the climax of blessing, the ultimate 'good thing' from God.

This 'Holy Spirit' principle will be extremely helpful when you think about the different promises that God made to Old Testament believers. It will make sure that you don't take any *inessential* Old Covenant conditions and promises – and wrongly apply them to yourself.

I hope, my friend, that you're beginning to understand the true and binding nature of God's New Covenant with you. But remember, it doesn't begin or end with you – His blessings extend to a thousand generations.

4

God blesses a thousand generations

The love of God is utterly unconditional. There's nothing that anyone can do to earn even the tiniest scrap.

When God sets His love on a person, He does so without a single condition. His love is always totally free and completely undemanding.

This means, dear friend, that God's New Covenant with you is full of *grace*. It's simply God's free and sovereign choice to fill you with His abundant divine favour.

> *"My kindness shall not depart from you, nor shall my covenant of peace be removed,"* says the Lord, *who has mercy on you.* Isaiah 54:10

When God makes a promise, He keeps it. This is His unchanging nature, for He's the faith*full* God.

His favour, however, doesn't last for just one lifetime, and it's not for only one generation, for He's the faithful, multi-generational God.

> *He is God, the faithful God who keeps covenant and mercy for a thousand generations with those who love Him and keep His commandments.*
> Deuteronomy 7:9

My dear friend, God plans to bless you to overflowing. And He intends that this will overflow to your family – and down through the generations.

It's time for you to understand this promise, and to learn how to claim it for yourself, for your children – and for your children's children!

Faithful God – unfaithful people!

In this book, I tell a few stories about some people who've heard God's Word, turned from their sins and started to enjoy His covenant promises. Sadly, not everyone we know responds to God in this wonderful way. Life's not that straightforward!

You can probably think of some people near you who simply don't want to know God. No matter what you say or do, they want nothing to do with your Jesus.

Don't give up on them, my friend. God is faithful to a thousand generations of those who love Him! He will lovingly pursue them and bring them to Himself – even if He has to use a little gracious discipline.

A certain Christian mother had a son who grew more and more rebellious. Eventually, the son was taken over by drug abuse and became totally immersed in the negative aspects of the modern music scene.

But the mother never gave up hope. She kept on pressing the Lord with His promises of salvation for her son.

One night, when the son's spiritual condition seemed as desperate as ever, God gave him a dream. He saw Jesus extending His arms to him; and the young man, now almost thirty, realised for the first time how his lifestyle was hurting the Lord who'd died to save him.

When he woke, he was a new person – totally born again. He turned his back on his sinful lifestyle and joined the music team of his church.

So never give up on your family, dear friend. God *will* find a way of reaching them!

God has no plan B

God always keeps His side of a covenant no matter what the other party does. When He created Adam and Eve, He intended that they should enjoy rich fellowship with Him. But they betrayed Him.

God didn't then decide to disown them and move on to 'plan B' – for there's never a 'plan B' with God. Instead, God immediately provided the way of redemption so that they could be restored.

God never scraps His plans, my friend. He never gives up – and He won't give up with a single member of your family.

God's covenant with Israel

We see the same pattern throughout the Old Testament. God blessed Israel according to His covenant, His binding agreement, with them. Yet

Israel and Judah backslid and turned to other gods.

God, however, never gave up on His people. He sent His prophets to reprove them, His judgements to chastise them, and gently encouraged them back to Him.

Even when they were exiled to Babylon, God did not forsake His people. Instead, He raised leaders to restore them to the promised land.

One such person was Nehemiah, whom God sent to rebuild the walls of Jerusalem. Nehemiah's first prayer praised God for His covenant faithfulness.

I pray, Lord God of heaven, O great and awesome God, You who keep Your covenant and mercy with those who love You and observe Your commandments... Nehemiah 1:7

This covenant was the basis of the great restoration which followed in Israel. God is faithful – even when we're not. He has His way of bringing us back to His holy plan and purpose.

My dear friend, God can reach out to your family; He can restore the most distant backslider; He can save even the most hardened sinner. Remember, His infinite mercy extends to a thousand generations of those who love Him.

The promise is for *your* family

God's mercy is going to pursue you all the days of your life! And this same mercy will be extended to all within your family bloodline.

Mercy will follow your unsaved husband, your separated wife, your rebellious son, even your long-lost daughter.

God will pursue your mother and your father: He will keep on pursuing them until they come to Him in repentance and faith.

In the next chapter, you'll learn how God's covenant with one man affects you. You'll see how a single covenant promise, made thousands of years ago, set God's blessing to you in motion.

Remember, the promise belongs to you – and to your family – forever!

5

God's covenant with Abram

About 4,000 years ago, in a remote part of the Middle East, God made a binding agreement with an elderly nomad.

Even though the man, Abram, didn't have any children, the covenant God made was not for him alone. Some aspects of the agreement were personal to Abram, but God's real intention was to bless the whole world through him.

The Lord first appeared to Abram in his native Mesopotamia, and told him to travel to a new land which would be revealed to him.

Together with his family, Abram walked about 600 miles to the city of Haran, where they stayed for several years.

God appeared to Abram again when he was 75 years old, and told him to leave Haran and travel to Canaan – which was 600 miles south-west.

God promised Abram:

I will bless you and make your name great; and you shall be a blessing... in you all the families of the earth shall be blessed.   **Genesis 12:2-3**

About 24 years later – when Abram was living in Canaan but was still childless – God repeated His promise. He renamed him Abraham, and commanded him to circumcise himself and his male descendants.

(Circumcision was a sign of the covenant and a reminder that the promises were to Abram *and* to all his descendants.)

In this way, God called Abraham, his family (including Lot, his nephew), his children (including Isaac) and his children's children (including Jacob, the head of the twelve tribes of Israel) and all his descendants thereafter.

Abram and Lot

When we look at Lot, we can see how he benefited from the covenant that God made with his uncle.

The blessing of God was so great that the land was unable to sustain them both. Abram graciously allowed Lot to choose which part of Canaan he wanted for himself.

Lot chose the plains near the Jordan river, so Abram had to settle in the less-fertile wilderness area to the west.

Abram dwelt in the land of Canaan, and Lot dwelt in the cities of the plain and pitched his tent even as far as Sodom Genesis 13:12

This was a dangerous move by Lot, because the people of the plains – which included Sodom and Gomorrah – were exceedingly wicked and sinful.

Another twenty years passed, and God sent two angels to Sodom to see just how evil it was.

When they reached the city, they witnessed such great wickedness they knew that judgement time had come. They had to fulfil the commission that God had given them to destroy the city.

But before they could do anything, they had to rescue Lot. One of the angels told Lot to hurry to a place of safety. Look at the reason the angel gave.

For I cannot do anything until you arrive there.
                                              Genesis 19:22

What a staggering statement! The angel of judgement could not destroy Sodom until Lot was in a place of safety! Why was this?

It was to do with the covenant! God had promised Abram that his family would be blessed, and God was simply keeping His covenant. It was God's mercy and favour, which had come upon Abram's family through the covenant, that saved Lot.

What a merciful God! Just think about it. God's blessing upon Abram overflowed to his family, so that even the fleshly and reluctant Lot was blessed.

God rescued Lot, and his family, and would not begin the judgement of Sodom and Gomorrah until they were safely out of the way.

God blesses them for *your* sake

My dear friend, your family may have no idea just how much they owe to your faith!

You've been brought into the New Covenant by faith in the blood of Jesus. And the blessings of this covenant overflow from your life to those close to you. They're blessed because of you!

Look again and see what a great miracle this was for Lot. He wasn't interested in spiritual things, and was very reluctant to leave his home. In fact, Lot had to be dragged out of his home by the angels!

Then he was told to flee with his family to the mountains. But instead of going, Lot began to argue with the angels! He wanted to run to another city, rather than obey them and head for the mountains.

Since Lot's life had just been saved, and divine judgement was about to fall, you'd think that Lot would have said, 'Yes sir! Thank you Sir! Where? The mountains? OK! We're outta here!'

You'd also think that the angels' patience would have been exhausted. Instead, an angel said:

I have favoured you concerning this thing also, in that I will not overthrow this city for which you have spoken. Hurry, escape there. Genesis 19:21

Lot's family lived under God's favour because of God's covenant with his uncle. And, when they went to the city of Zoar, that city did not fall!

Do you see what happened? The blessing which had flowed from Abram to Lot then overflowed from Lot to the people of Zoar!

The angels were legally bound to save Abram's extended family – even his nephew and his nephew's children! Despite his sinful reluctance, Lot was saved. And all because of God's unbreakable covenant with Abram!

Remember Lot's wife

Lot's story should fill you with much peace about the spiritual state of your loved ones.

You can probably think of some relatives who appear to follow Christ rather reluctantly. They never seem to be whole-hearted in their Christian commitment.

God's great care for Abram's relatives should help you to appreciate that He will take strong action to save your loved ones – *if* there's the tiniest response on their part.

The New Covenant, however, doesn't mean that all your relatives will be saved *automatically*. They must be willing to take a decisive step for themselves.

Remember Lot's wife! She disobeyed the angel by looking back at Sodom – and died.

You can be blessed because of someone else's faith, but you can't be saved by someone else's faith. You must believe for yourself.

If you're reading this book, and think that you're a Christian because one of your parents is a believer – you're mistaken. Don't think for one second that the faith of anyone else will benefit you on the day when you meet Jesus face to face.

There's only one way to be sure about your salvation. That's for you to believe for yourself – for you to trust Jesus personally as your Saviour and Lord.

Don't delay! Get right with God today. Don't put it off to tomorrow. *Today is the acceptable time!*

When you do believe, however, you stand in line to receive all the blessings of God. And you bring this blessing into your family – even to your nieces and nephews and their children.

The holy covenant you enter by faith in Jesus benefits your entire family, your whole household – in exactly the same way as Abram's covenant with God benefited his extended family.

6

Family salvation

Family salvation is a much bigger biblical theme than most people realise. When you grasp that God really does have a special interest in saving your extended family, your whole approach will change.

You'll begin to have genuine hope for those members of your family who seem to be far away from God.

You'll stop pleading blindly for the salvation of your loved ones, and will start pressing your case boldly in the heavenlies by bringing God's covenant promises before Him.

You'll know that every member of your household is the object of God's special intentions – you'll be sure that He's watching over them for an opportunity to press home His claims.

And, instead of desperately trying to push your family into commitment, you'll be able to present them with a loving, confident, consistent witness – because you'll know that the covenant-keeping, multi-generational God is in control!

Noah

It's a basic biblical principle that God's grace is most present where it's most needed.

Where sin abounded, grace abounded even much more. Romans 5:20

This was certainly true in Noah's day. The people of Noah's generation were so wicked that God was sorry He'd ever put humankind on the earth.

The Lord saw that the wickedness of man was great in the earth, and that every intent of the thoughts of his heart was only evil continually.
Genesis 6:5

Noah, however, found grace in the eyes of the Lord! God's grace was poured into his life and he was declared righteous before the Holy God.

There's only one way for you to be counted righteous, dear friend, and that's by grace. If His grace fills your life, the blessing of deliverance is bound to follow – and it will overflow to your family around you.

When Noah received grace, it touched his family! God instructed him to build an ark which would carry him to safety. But the ark was not for Noah alone. The same gracious deliverance was extended to his children and in-laws.

The Lord said to Noah, 'Come into the ark, you and all your household, because I have seen that you are righteous before Me in this generation'.
Genesis 7:1

Is it possible for God to treat your family like this, my friend? Do you think God will show the same mercy to your family that He showed to Noah's?

Of course He will! He has not changed. In blessing you, God desires to extend exactly the same blessing to those around you – to your family!

The family passover

When God instituted the passover feast for Israel, He was preparing to send the last of the ten plagues to Egypt. He was about to strike the first-born in the land.

God's covenant with Abraham guaranteed that He would keep His people safe. But how would He do this? The divine instruction soon came:

Every man shall take for himself a lamb… a lamb for a household. Exodus 12:3

This was to be a family passover. There was to be one lamb for each household. Once again, God was extending His grace on a family basis.

The lamb was killed and eaten by the family: there was enough for them all to enjoy. And the blood of the lamb was sprinkled over the doorposts and lintel of their home – family by family, household by household.

Look at the significance of this statement:

When I see the blood, I shall pass over you; and the plague shall not be on you to destroy you when I strike the land of Egypt. Exodus 12:13

This is good news for our families! It shows that the blood of Jesus – our passover Lamb – benefits our household, and not just us individually.

Dear friend, this very important Old Testament picture should start to convince you that God wants to save your whole family.

Rahab's family

Rahab the harlot is one of the greatest biblical examples of household salvation.

Together with the other people in Jericho, Rahab had heard about God drying the Red Sea for the people of Israel, and she'd learnt about their recent victory over the Amorites. Now the people of God were camped outside Jericho!

Joshua sent two spies to check the city defences, and they came to the harlot's house. When the king of Jericho heard about this, he demanded that Rahab turn the spies over to him. Instead, she hid them on the roof and deceived the king's men.

First, Rahab explained her actions to the spies:

I know that the Lord has given you the land, that the terror of you has fallen on us. Joshua 2:9

FAMILY SALVATION

Then she asked the spies to spare her – along with her whole family:

Spare my father, my mother, my brothers, my sisters and all they have, and deliver our lives from death. Joshua 2:13

Can you see the principle that's being established? God is interested in your *whole family*. He wants them all to be saved and to enjoy the blessings of His New Covenant.

The spies agreed to Rahab's requests, and told her to tie a red cord in her window. This would identify Rahab's house to the army of Israel.

The spies kept their promise. When the walls of Jericho fell, the army of Israel descended on the city. As soon as they saw the red cord hanging from Rahab's window, they made sure that *all* the people in that house were kept safe.

What a marvellous story! And what an encouragement for you to trust God for your household to be saved!

The red cord should remind you of the blood of Jesus which pleads for your family. His blood has power over your whole household. God will work in the life of *every member* of your family.

Although the members of Rahab's household were protected *corporately* from the invading army, they all had to trust the spies' promise of safety *individually*.

The family listened together to Rahab's warnings, and then each member personally believed the promise of salvation that she'd received from the spies. When the time came, they all chose to take refuge under Rahab's roof.

After this, Rahab and her family were incorporated into the people of God. Their old life in Jericho was forgotten. The harlot became a mother in Israel. She even became an ancestor of king David – and so of Jesus, the Messiah!

A house for David

For many years, King David had a secret dream: he wanted to build God a house. It was a noble idea and David clung to it passionately.

The time came when David's battles against his enemies were over, and David shared his dream with Nathan the prophet. Nathan thought that it was a good idea – until God spoke to him.

God told Nathan that it wasn't for David to build Him a house. Instead, God promised Nathan that He would make David a house – not a building; a seed, a dynasty, a kingdom 'forever'.

God's plans were bigger and better than David's dreams. The king wanted to build God a physical monument; but the Lord had a much better idea.

God wanted to create a royal bloodline, a holy dynasty which would last for generations, a special family which would result in the coming of Jesus – great David's greater Son!

In the meantime, David's dream would be fulfilled – not by himself, but by one of his sons. David's heir, Solomon, would take up the call to build the Temple.

God plans for the long term

Most of us think in the short term – we focus on the immediate – whereas God thinks about the future: He always works out *long-term* plans.

God's plans for our lives don't have to do only with ourselves and the people around us. He's also concerned with our descendants.

Our plans are far too small when they extend only to our own lifetimes. It's much better to make sure that we align ourselves with His plans for us – for these will affect the generations to come.

Many things, my friend, which may be just a dream in your life will be made real by the 'Solomons' who come after you. This is why you must be faithful to God's covenant purposes.

You must discover God's principle purpose for your life, and fulfil it. When you do this, you'll set up a chain of blessing which will affect the generations who come after you.

This is *a vital principle* of the Holy Spirit. God deals with you as an individual, but He doesn't stop there. He sees you as part of a much larger picture.

None of us can know what purposes of God pivot on our obedience.

Can you imagine what would have happened if Abram had refused to leave Haran? Or if Noah had decided not to build the ark? Or if the people of Israel had not bothered to sacrifice their lambs?

Why, the history of every family on earth would have been different!

It's the same in your life, dear friend. Your loving obedience to God's call on your life doesn't affect only you – it also affects future generations in ways which are beyond your wildest imagination!

The call of God is never revoked

Are you convinced yet that God causes *whole families* to be blessed?

He calls and He chooses; and His call is never revoked. God even passes His call on to future generations so that His will is *completely* fulfilled.

Although Acts 7:2 shows that God spoke to Abram in Mesopotamia, Genesis 11:27-32 suggests that it was Abram's father who was called to leave the country and travel to Canaan – over 1,000 miles away.

Terah took his son Abram and his grandson Lot... and his daughter-in-law Sarai... and they went out with them from Ur of the Chaldeans to go to the land of Canaan; and they came to Haran and dwelt there.   Genesis 11:31

Terah seems to have followed the river Euphrates north-west for 600 miles, and then stopped at Haran. He got half-way to Canaan, half-way to God's purposes, and then went no further.

It was only after Terah died in Haran that God called his son, Abram, to fulfil *completely* His purposes for the family. Praise God, Abram went all the way to Canaan!

God still works in this same *multi-generational* way, and calls children to fulfil what their parents failed to complete.

About sixty-five years ago in Nakuru, Kenya, a young boy was close to death. His mother, the wife of a farmer, was desperate – for children died easily in Kenya in those days. She was a staunch believer in Jesus, and knew that only a miracle could save her son's life.

As the mother cried out to the Lord, she promised that – if God healed her son – she would dedicate him to serve the Lord.

God answered her prayers, and the boy lived. He grew up, married and had a family of his own.

Although the son knew God, he chose not to walk with Him. He never took up the call of God on his life, and died without serving God.

But God didn't forget the covenant that had been made with the mother – and He looked to the next generation to fulfil it completely.

Within a year of the man's death as an adult, his second son became a Christian and dedicated himself to serve God. The covenant was honoured. The Holy Spirit then called this second son to do what his father had been unwilling to do.

That was me! I know that I owe my destiny in ministry to my grandmother's promise when her son's life hung on a thread.

I hope, my dear friend, you now understand that God wants to save your household *and* that He's been dealing with you and your family across the generations.

Pause for a while again. Reflect on God's purposes for your family. Think through exactly what this means for your life. And ask God to show you exactly what action you need to take.

7

New Covenant promises

Some people disregard the biblical stories that we've read. They say that the Old Testament isn't relevant any more, and that we shouldn't apply its stories to our lives today.

You've seen, however, that God didn't cancel the blessings of the Old Covenant when He made the New Covenant. But this doesn't mean that there are no differences between the two covenants.

The Old Covenant was meant to bless the nation of Israel; whereas the New Covenant benefits all who believe – whatever their nationality.

The people of Israel received the blessings of the Old Covenant by obeying the Law, whereas we receive the blessings of the New Covenant by grace through faith.

The Old Covenant was repeatedly sealed with the blood of bulls and goats, whereas our New Covenant was sealed once-and-for-all with the precious blood of Jesus.

But do these differences mean that God has broken or forgotten His Old Covenant promises? Of course not! The essential blessings of the Old Testament are still available for New Testament believers – they're for you and your family.

Higher dimension blessing

When God makes a fresh covenant, He doesn't destroy the old one. Instead, He adds to the first and takes it to a higher level.

If God was interested in families in the old order under Moses, don't you think that He's still concerned with them today?

Jesus, the Mediator of the New Covenant, came to reveal the Father to us. And God's fatherhood – His 'family nature' – extends over all His people.

God does not change. He is the same yesterday, today and forever. If He set His love upon households in Old Testament times, you can be certain that He sets His love on households today.

If He wanted to bless the families of His Old Testament people, you can be sure that He wants to bless the families of His New Testament people.

You've already read, dear friend, that all God's promises – old *and* new – are fulfilled in Christ.

He has blessed us with every spiritual blessing in the heavenly places in Christ   Ephesians 1:3

Look how clearly Paul expresses this in another letter to New Covenant believers.

All the promises of God in Him are Yes, and in Him Amen.   2 Corinthians 1:20

There's *more* in Christ

There's no suggestion in the New Testament that God has discarded His Old Testament promises. Instead, He's gathered them together and placed them *in Christ*.

Jesus fulfilled the Father's will perfectly, and shed His blood on the cross, to seal the New Covenant. This means that we're set to receive *every blessing* that God has by the Spirit who works in our hearts.

The Holy Spirit is the crowning blessing of the Old and New Covenants. He comes loaded with *all* the benefits of God and pours them into our lives.

You've nothing to fear, my friend, and nothing to lose. God is faithful to *all His covenant promises*.

The New Testament records many examples of God fulfilling His covenant promise of household salvation. These biblical examples should convince you that the essential blessings of the Old Covenant still apply today.

A dishonest tax collector

Jericho's chief tax collector had become wealthy by collecting taxes dishonestly. This made the man, Zacchaeus, very unpopular in the town.

One day, as Jesus was passing through Jericho, He called to Zacchaeus and told him that He was coming to his home.

HOUSEHOLD SALVATION

Many of the local people who heard this were dreadfully upset. How could Jesus enter the home of such a terrible sinner!

The people didn't realise that Jesus was the friend of sinners, and that this visit was a gracious sign of His love and acceptance.

This overflowing love broke every barrier in Zacchaeus' heart; it even convicted him of his greed. He said to Jesus:

Lord, I give half my goods to the poor; and if I have taken anything from anyone by false accusation, I restore fourfold. Luke 19:8

Look carefully at the effect that Zacchaeus' repentance had on his family:

Jesus said to him, 'Today salvation has come into this house, because he also is a son of Abraham'.
Luke 19:8

The blessing of salvation, which was poured onto Zacchaeus that day, was a fulfilment of God's promise to Abraham. And it overflowed to all the people in Zacchaeus' house: it was *household salvation*.

Every person in Zacchaeus' family was touched as a result of his repentance. It released the gift of salvation into his whole household.

A devout soldier

The New Testament reports that Cornelius was a Roman centurion who was faithful both in his giving to the poor and in his praying to God. He was a devout soldier who feared God – together with all his household.

God sent an angel to bring Cornelius into the full knowledge of the gospel so that he might be saved. The angel instructed him to send for Peter from a nearby town.

Cornelius called his household together and they waited for the apostle to come.

When Peter arrived, Cornelius spoke in anticipation:

We are all present before God, to hear all the things commanded you by God. Acts 10:33

Peter preached to the whole company. They all believed the gospel, and the Holy Spirit fell on them even before Peter had finished his sermon.

Can you see how the Spirit dealt with them as a family? They didn't get saved one by one – they all came together. It's wonderful when this happens today. It's a glorious fulfilment of household salvation.

Of course, not every family gets saved in a single meeting! You can be sure, however, that the Lord who touched Cornelius' family according to His covenant purposes is also at work in your family.

A distraught jailer

Paul and Silas had been witnessing in Philippi. There'd been several converts, but a slave girl had been giving them trouble.

She was possessed by an evil spirit and could make psychic predictions – which brought great profit to her owners. This young girl kept on disturbing the open-air meetings that Paul and Silas were holding in the market.

Paul finally acted, and God set the girl free. Her owners were furious, as their means of income had been taken away. They dragged Paul and Silas before the magistrates, and had them thrown into the town jail.

But God was at work! At midnight, when Paul and Silas were singing praises and praying, God sent an earthquake. The jail shook. The doors burst open. The prisoners were free.

Instead of escaping, however, Paul and Silas stayed behind to preach to the jailer. This was his response:

Sirs, what must I do to be saved? Acts 16:30

Paul replied:

Believe on the Lord Jesus Christ, and you will be saved, you and your household. Acts 16:31

Do you see that Paul did not appeal just to the individual? He directed his message to the whole family. Later that night, the jailer's entire household heard the gospel, believed, and were baptised.

My dear friend, when you're speaking to one member of a family about Christ, think about the whole family. Direct your witnessing to *whole families*. You'll be surprised how often God honours His promises to the household.

If you're the only believer in your family, begin to believe God for the other members of your family.

Remember, God keeps covenant with families. This means that you can pray with boldness for the salvation of *all* the members of your family.

Speak to them with confidence about Christ. Show them your faith by your actions. Shower them with love, grace and patience. This will provide God with a powerful base for the covenant-keeping operation of His Spirit. He will work to fulfil His promises. He will not fail you.

The promise of the Spirit

The gift of the Holy Spirit is the greatest of all God's covenant promises: every other promise finds its ultimate fulfilment in this one.

The presence of God's Spirit in your life is the very purpose of your salvation. You're now in direct contact – in a living relationship – with God Himself.

But what about your family and household? Do they have a share in the Spirit, or are they excluded from the covenant goodness of God? Of course not!

In one of the strongest New Testament passages on the subject, God shows how His covenant promises are going to be fulfilled in your family.

He reveals that the promise of the Spirit is not just for you, it's also for your children! In fact, it's for *all* whom the Lord will call.

Repent and let every one of you be baptised in the name of Jesus Christ for the remission of sins; and you shall receive the gift of the Holy Spirit.

For the promise is to you and to your children, and to all who are afar off, as many as the Lord our God will call. Acts 2:38-39

My dear friend, look closely at the context of these words. They're spoken by Peter at the beginning of the church age. They come at the end of the very first sermon to be preached in the New Testament age of the Spirit.

Jesus has returned to heaven. The Spirit has come. The crowds have gathered to hear Peter preach the gospel. This is *a Christian sermon*, my friend; it belongs to the New Covenant. It's not a Jewish sermon spoken under the Old Covenant.

In this, the first Christian sermon, we see how God's Old Testament promises of household salvation and family blessing apply to us in the church. God still has a blessing for families. He promises the Holy Spirit to us *and to our children!*

This means that it really is God's will for His salvation to touch your entire family. He does not call just you to come to faith and receive the Spirit – He calls your children too.

In one of his letters, the Apostle Paul gives an example of this. Genuine faith dwelt in a gentile woman called Lois; then in her daughter, Eunice; and then in her grandson, Timothy. God did not call and bless only the grandmother – He called her child and grandchild too!

Of course, as with Eunice and Timothy, each member of your family must make their personal response to the gospel. There must be individual repentance and individual faith: we cannot live by our grandparents' faith. Nevertheless, God clearly promises to be especially present in your family.

He longs to fulfil His covenant promise to your household. He takes every opportunity to call them and speak to them by His Spirit. He actively pursues them, and will stay outside their lives only if they wilfully resist Him.

But remember, dear friend, the Holy Spirit can penetrate the most hardened hearts. He can reach every single member of your family with His great love and power.

8

Strongholds come down

You've seen that God's promises overflow to your families and descendants. This means that He's saying to you, my friend, 'Because of your faith, I'm going to respect your family. I'm going to bless them. My grace will flow from you into their lives.'

This may sound fine in theory, but you're probably saying, 'You haven't met *my* family!' Perhaps you've been praying for them for years, and they seem no closer to knowing Jesus than they've ever been.

But God knows the opposition which is trying to prevent you from experiencing His promises – and He's made full provision to deal with it.

God will equip you

Jesus has promised that the Holy Spirit will come alongside you to help you, to strengthen you, and to guide you into all truth. And God is calling you to keep on being filled with the Spirit so that His purposes can be fulfilled in your life.

Jesus guarantees that, when you live close to Him every day, He will equip you for the battle.

Of course, the devil resists God's plans all the time; but God will give you all the spiritual weapons you need to overcome the enemy.

Don't resort to your own plans and tactics. These always fail. Instead, ask the Lord to give you *His wisdom* and *His determination* to pursue His covenant promises for your family.

The weapons of our warfare are not carnal, but mighty in God for the pulling down of strongholds, casting down arguments, and every high thing that exalts itself against the knowledge of God, bringing every thought into captivity to the obedience of Christ.   2 Corinthians 10:4-5

Remember, dear friend, the Bible promises that God will give you the spiritual means to break every obstacle, and to overthrow every stronghold which is opposing the will of God for your family.

When you live your life in the presence of God, your family and friends will see the blessings of God in your life.

Witness wisely

Your parents may have been good Christians who helped you to start trusting Jesus when you were young. This is a great blessing; and it's one that you can pass on to your own children.

Or it may be that you're the first member of your family to come to Christ. If this is so, the change in your life can make a dramatic impact on your household. They'll witness the Holy Spirit's work and see the difference He makes. You could be the first link in the chain of blessing which will pass down the generations.

Make sure, however, that you don't bash your family with Bible texts! Let your new life do the witnessing!

Back in the 1950's, a young woman accepted Jesus and joined a church youth group. At first, she was rather aggressive in her witness to her family; and this caused her mother to become hostile.

Eventually, the girl realised that actions speak louder than words. Her Bible bashing gave way to a more gentle witness, and she clung to the promises of God. It took time; but, thirty years later, her mother accepted Christ. Hallelujah!

God sanctifies your spouse

In the days of the early church, people from pagan families started to follow Christ. This prompted all sorts of questions among the new believers. Should they leave their ungodly households? Should they divorce their unbelieving partners?

Paul taught them that they'd nothing to fear.

The unbelieving husband is sanctified by the wife, and the unbelieving wife is sanctified by the husband.   1 Corinthians 7:14

If your spouse is not a believer, my friend, realise that – in God's eyes – *they're sanctified by you!*

Wow! I can already hear your reaction! 'You mean that pagan husband of mine is sanctified? You must be joking! I *know* the man!'

I understand your reaction, but God doesn't see him the way that you do. *God sees him as he's going to be!* Hallelujah!

God has His long-term ways of bringing people round, and He pursues the unsaved husbands and wives of believers with exceptional keenness.

Do you know why this is? It's because the unsaved partners of believers *are* sanctified. They're set apart for God and marked out as prime candidates for salvation.

Maybe, dear friend, you've been trying *too* hard to get your spouse saved. Forget it! Start believing God instead. Begin to see your partner as sanctified and love them accordingly – love them into the kingdom.

'But', you say, 'how can I do this? I've tried for so long and nothing seems to change.'

Look to the long-term, my friend, and remember that love always wins through in the end.

Don't give up. Wives, keep on ironing your husband's shirts neatly and promptly; husbands, do the washing up everyday and share in the cleaning; and pray for them as you iron their clothes and wash their dishes.

Don't get so spiritual that your partner can't relate to you any more. Keep your feet on the earth. Never judge your partner.

And remember, the best way of witnessing is by allowing Christ to make you the best wife, the best husband, that you can be. You'll win your partner to Jesus when you show them Jesus' life-long, unceasing, unchanging love.

A restored marriage

A woman I know had been asking the Lord to restore her broken marriage. She'd tried many times to be reconciled to her non-Christian husband. But the more she tried to be a godly wife, the worse the relationship became. Finally, her husband left home yet again.

His wife, however, was determined to trust God and she asked Him to show her the next step. She stopped trying to persuade her husband, and held him before the Lord in prayer.

She took a job in a Christian organisation and became active in the church. This was a special time, and she affirmed God's love for her children and grew in her relationship with God.

Meanwhile, her husband was still living in the same town. As time went by, it seemed as though he met Christians everywhere he went! One of them told him that only Jesus could take away all the hurt caused by his broken marriage.

They invited him to church and he committed his life to Christ. Soon, he realised that he wanted his family back more than anything else. With the support of his new Christian friends, he began to pray for Jesus to work things out.

The long process of reconciliation began until finally their marriage was healed. They began to see their home blossom in peace and harmony.

In this new environment of love, their children turned to Christ for themselves. Praise God that this is far from a unique story!

If you're going through some deep marital or family distress, dear friend, let me assure you that you *can* trust God. Don't give up hope. Don't stop praying. Don't turn your back on God's covenant promises for your family.

God will honour your faith and your patient perseverance.

9

Promises for your family

You've seen, my friend, how God's covenant works. Just as in Old Testament times, He wills to touch *whole families* with His goodness and love.

You've learnt that the Old Covenant promises have been *extended* in the New Covenant. They're no longer limited to physical blessings; instead, they've been extended to include the fullness of the spiritual realm.

This means that God now fulfils His covenant promises to you in-and-through the Holy Spirit.

You've also understood that the people of Israel benefited from the Old Covenant only by obeying the Law of Moses; whereas we enjoy God's New Covenant blessings by His grace through our faith in His Son – who fulfilled the Law quite perfectly.

Because of Christ, you're free from the Law, with all its demands and penalties. In place of these, you've an unbreakable covenant right to all the promises of God.

Every promise of God has been signed, sealed and bound to you, my friend, by the blood of Jesus – the blood of the New Covenant.

Living faith

We receive and enjoy the blessings of God's covenant promises by *living faith*.

This means believing, trusting and acting on the promises that Jesus has secured for you by His death on the cross.

Living faith recognises that these spiritual realities are accomplished truths, and it receives them into the realm of human experience.

The blessings of the New Covenant, therefore, are not automatic for you, dear friend; rather, you must 'faith' them, or 'believe' them, into your life.

This means that you must know what promises are available for you and your family. After all, if you don't know what He's promised, you won't be able to believe His promises!

Many people long for their families to be saved and to come into the fullness of the Holy Spirit. But they don't know the promises of God in these matters, and sit back merely hoping that God will do something.

You can't truly lay hold of God for something, unless you know that it's His will to give it to you.

The covenant and your family

When believers begin to see their unsaved families in the same way that God sees them, their whole approach is transformed.

- ⇒ Do you understand, dear friend, that your unsaved partner is precious to God?
- ⇒ Do you realise that God looks upon all your children as special objects of His care and protection?
- ⇒ Do you know that – even if you're the only believer in your family – your faith sanctifies the other members of your household?

Look carefully at this teaching of Paul:

The unbelieving husband is sanctified by the wife, and the unbelieving wife is sanctified by the husband; otherwise your children would be unclean, but now they are holy. 1 Corinthians 7:14

Go back over this amazing verse and read it phrase by phrase. Can you take it in? Can you see the wonderful implications for your family?

Covenant language

Did you notice the highly-charged covenant language? Paul says that your family is set apart to God for His covenant blessings.

Your unbelieving partner is 'sanctified' and your sinful children are made 'clean' by your faith. Instead of being outside the covenant, they're under its influence and deemed holy by God.

I guarantee that, when you grasp this truth, you'll never look at your family in the same way again!

You'll stop seeing them as hardened sinners who resist the gospel and ridicule your faith. And you'll start seeing them as ripe candidates for salvation, and ready targets for the blessing of God.

Covenant blessings

My dear friend, your faith in Christ has brought you into the overflowing blessings of the covenant. And, because you've been adopted as a covenant child of God, the members of your family have been exposed to the blessings of the covenant. They're in a very favourable position with God.

Think of the blessings which have come to you since you believed. Haven't they touched your family? If you've had joy, hasn't this blessed them? If you've had peace, hasn't this benefited them too?

And what about the physical blessings of God? When God has prospered you, hasn't this brought financial blessing to your household? When family members have been ill, hasn't your faith brought an element of healing – whether they believe it or not?

The real truth, dear friend, is that every single member of your family has been blessed in some way because of your faith.

The things which have happened to them are not circumstantial or accidental. They're deliberate and intentional. They're part of God's plan.

He's been passing on the blessings of the covenant to your loved ones because of your faith in His Son.

Spiritual blessings

Of course, the essential blessings of the New Covenant are spiritual, not physical.

The central benefits of the covenant are the gift of Christ's own righteousness, the privileged right of access to God's throne, the abiding presence of the Spirit in your life.

All these blessings must be received personally, but the unbelievers in your family have many spiritual advantages because you're among them.

For example, they're in a privileged position to hear the gospel; they've an opportunity to see God work close at hand; and they're ideally placed to experience God for themselves.

God's grace is near to bring your relatives to faith. But He cannot by-pass their responsibility to believe for themselves. All the advantages which come to your family through you must lead each member to a personal commitment to Christ.

A promise for your children

My dear friend, God has given you some very precious promises for your unsaved relatives. For example, He promises that all your children will be taught by the Lord and kept in peace and well-being.

All your children shall be taught by the Lord, and great shall be the peace of your children.
　　　　　　　　　　　　　　　　Isaiah 54:13

Best of all, this promise is not just for your children – it's for your grandchildren and great-grandchildren too!

'As for Me,' says the Lord, 'this is My covenant with them: My Spirit who is upon you, and My words which I have put in your mouth, shall not depart from your mouth, nor from the mouth of your descendants, nor from the mouth of your descendants' descendants,' says the Lord, 'from this time and forevermore.'　　　Isaiah 59:21

A promise for your spouse

The Bible makes it clear that Christians should not marry unbelievers. This protects us from much heartache and disappointment.

Unfortunately, some believers are in this situation. You may have compromised yourself in some way, or discovered that the person you married is not the Christian they claimed to be, or you may have become a Christian and your spouse hasn't yet accepted your faith.

God is very compassionate. He wants to establish blessing and harmony in your home; He already sees your unsaved spouse as 'sanctified'; and His Spirit is working to bring them to Christ.

In some situations, however, this promise seems very far from fulfilment.

This is why Peter calls wives to win their unsaved husbands by godly and submissive behaviour, and husbands to win their unsaved wives by honouring and understanding them properly. Remember, dear friend, a Christ-like life speaks louder than words.

Wives, be submissive to your own husbands, that even if some do not obey the word, they, without a word, may be won by the conduct of their wives....

Husbands, dwell with them with understanding, giving honour to the wife... that your prayers may not be hindered.   1 Peter 3:1-7

Of course, these promises don't bypass your partner's personal responsibility. They must believe in Jesus for themselves. But God's Word gives you enormous encouragement to believe for the salvation and restoration of your unsaved partner.

A promise for backsliders

God hasn't forgotten the people in your family who've backslid. He promises to send His Spirit to draw them back to Himself.

Thus says the Lord: 'Refrain your voice from weeping, and your eyes from tears; for your work shall be rewarded', says the Lord, 'and they shall come back from the land of the enemy'.

'There is hope in your future', says the Lord, 'that your children shall come back to their own border'. Jeremiah 31:16-17

We go through a heartbreaking time when one of our loved ones backslides. It's terrible to see a brother or sister, a wife or husband, a son or daughter, turn away from the Lord and fall back into sin.

Nobody is more unhappy than a backslider. They're under the Lord's chastisement and are cut off from all that they knew of God's goodness and blessing.

This can make them very hard to live with! They don't want a reminder of what they've left. And they do everything they can to avoid the convicting influence of the Holy Spirit.

But Jesus is very gracious. He's the good Shepherd who goes on searching for His lost and straying sheep until He finds them. He promises to restore those who wander away. And He will bring all His children to perfection and present them complete before His Father.

He who has begun a good work in you will complete it until the day of Jesus Christ.
Philippians 1:6

Dear friend, let the Lord's goodness and patience bring the backsliders in your family to repentance. Don't strive or be anxious. Don't pressurise them or try and make them feel guilty. Pray for them, don't preach at them!

God will restore them, not you. He is faithful. He will keep His covenant promises. He will answer your prayers for your family members.

10

Praying for your family

By now, dear friend, you should have begun to appreciate the wonderful promises that God has given for your family.

⇒ You know that He doesn't want anyone to perish – especially those in a household of faith.

⇒ You realise that He blesses you so that His blessings overflow to the people around you.

⇒ You understand that your partner is sanctified because of your faith.

⇒ You appreciate that the promise of the Spirit is for your children as well as for you.

I trust, my friend, that you've been assured by the Word that God really is willing to save *every* single member of your family, and that He wills to save them all.

This means that you can *pray in faith* when you pray for the different members of your family – especially when you intercede for your unsaved loved ones.

Pray believing

In *Prayer That Gets Answers* (it's the first book in this LIVING WORD SERIES) I show how you can pray with the expectancy that God will answer your prayers.

Among other things, I stress how important it is for you to pray according to the will of God.

Well, my friend, you already know that it's God's will to save the lost. You can pray, therefore, with 100% certainty that it's His will for every single member of your family to be saved.

You can intercede with firm faith and bold belief that God will fulfil His covenant promise to you of household salvation. In your prayers, therefore, keep on reminding God of His Word. Press Him every day to act according to His covenant.

Sometimes the answer comes quickly – much sooner than you expect! At other times, God looks for the perseverance of your faith. Whatever happens for you, keep on praying. Never give up, for God will reward your diligence and faithfulness in His good 'long-term' time.

The blood pleads

Always remember Jesus' blood when you pray for your unsaved loved ones.

Just as Abel's blood cried for vengeance against one member of his family, so Jesus' blood pleads for salvation for all the members of your family.

His precious blood was shed in love for your loved ones, and now it pleads before God's throne that the purpose of its shedding be fulfilled.

This is the blood which gives you access into the Father's presence. While, in prayer, you're using this access to remind God of His covenant promises, the blood is itself pleading with Him for your loved ones. You can be sure that the perfect blood will not plead in vain!

There are four main things to do when you pray for the unsaved members of your family.

1. pray for yourself

Don't just pray endlessly for your loved ones to be saved. (God doesn't need any persuading to save them.) Pray also that:

⇒ *you'll know when to speak and when to be silent*

⇒ *you'll be equipped to answer their questions*

⇒ *you'll know what to do to help them believe*

⇒ *your life won't cause them to stumble*

⇒ *you'll be filled with Christ's patience and love*

2. pray for other believers

It's usually true that our loved ones are more likely to listen to someone outside the family than to us; so pray for the believers who naturally come into contact with them. Pray that they'll:

⇒ *be bold and sensitive in their witness*

⇒ *know exactly what to say – and what not to say!*

⇒ *reveal God's love and power*

⇒ *be good and loyal friends*

⇒ *be full of God's Spirit*

3. deal with the enemy

The devil's main aim is to keep people out of heaven, and he does this by blinding the minds of those who do not believe.

We were blinded like the rest. Yet the time came when our eyes were opened and we believed in Jesus. Someone was praying for us – and God's mercy penetrated our minds with the gospel.

If the enemy was defeated in our lives, then he can be defeated in our loved ones' lives. But we have to learn to fight for them in the Spirit.

God's weapons are effective against Satan's strategies. You can battle in the Spirit for the souls of your family. Cry to God for their deliverance. Stand against the devil's work in their lives.

Learn to take authority over the activity of the enemy. Forbid him from confusing your loved ones, from blinding and deceiving them, from distracting them with wrong passions, and so on.

Your loved ones must decide for themselves to follow God – your prayers cannot 'make them' trust Christ. But, through spiritual warfare, you can break Satan's hold over their minds so that they will listen to the gospel and decide for themselves.

4. remove any obstacles

If you spend time listening to God, you can receive His identification of any obstacles which are preventing your loved ones from being saved.

Ask God to show you the circumstances, factors, people and attitudes which are preventing the work of God from being accepted by your family.

Then, in prayer, address these obstacles and command them, 'to be taken up', 'to be moved', 'to be uprooted', and so on. You may need to intercede in this way for many months, perhaps even several years, until the obstacle is removed.

Have faith in God... Whoever says to this mountain, 'Be removed and be cast into the sea,' and does not doubt in his heart, but believes that those things he says will come to pass, he will have whatever he says. Mark 11:22-23

Win by love

It's most important, my dear friend, that you combine appropriate actions with your praying. Faith without works is dead! And prayers without matching actions are useless!

HOUSEHOLD SALVATION

You must share the gospel with those whom you want to be saved. Prayer alone is not enough. Seek for the right moment, and speak to them sensitively about Christ.

But remember, the most effective way of witnessing is showing them your good deeds and your consistent Christ-like life over a considerable period of time.

Pause now, and make this prayer declaration for your household. Read it carefully, think about the different members of your family, and then declare it audibly – with bold faith.

"Father, I thank you that my whole family is underneath Your blessing.

"I now lay claim to all Your promises of Household Salvation. Release Your healing, Your deliverance and Your full salvation into every member of my family.

"I declare that every negative influence, and all demonic powers relating to my family, are overthrown in the mighty name of Jesus.

"As for me and my house, we will serve the Lord! Amen."

11

Blessings and curses

My dear friend, if you long for your family to experience and to enjoy God's overflowing blessings, you need to understand what the Bible teaches about blessings and curses.

The Old Testament shows that blessings and curses both operate at a family and at a multi-generational level.

The Lord is long-suffering and abundant in mercy, forgiving iniquity and transgression; but He by no means clears the guilty, visiting the iniquity of the fathers on the children to the third and fourth generation.   Numbers 14:18

> *For I, the Lord your God, am a jealous God, visiting the iniquity of the fathers upon the children to the third and fourth generations of those who hate Me, but showing mercy to thousands, to those who love Me and keep My commandments.* Deuteronomy 5:9-10

These Old Testament verses underline the fact that God is loving and merciful. He is gracious and forgiving – but He will not ignore your sin, or hold back its effects, if you refuse to repent.

These verses also reveal that blessing and curses can effect succeeding generations. The sins of the fathers are visited upon their children to the third and fourth generations; whereas God's blessing lasts a thousand generations!

Truly, my friend, God is ready to bless you and reluctant to curse you!

What are blessings?

All true blessing comes from God, and He blesses your family because this is His holy nature.

> *He... is the blessed and only Potentate, the King of kings and Lord of lords.* 1 Timothy 6:15

BLESSINGS AND CURSES

Whenever God blesses, He imparts something of Himself. As the only Lord over all, His blessing is supreme. Not even the devil can resist it!

God blesses you graciously and sovereignly, dear friend, according to His own good purpose. You can't force Him to bless you, and you can't snatch a blessing from His hand. Even so, it's His loving nature to pour overflowing blessings on all those who're willing to receive them.

God blesses through the Word of His mouth on the breath of His Spirit: He *pronounces* blessing. This means that we're blessed when God speaks, or breathes, His blessing into our lives.

The book of Deuteronomy lists many of the Old Covenant blessings. (You can read them in Deuteronomy 8:13-15 and 28:1-14.) These include:

⇒ *fertility*

⇒ *health*

⇒ *victory*

⇒ *prosperity*

⇒ *good reputation*

⇒ *family harmony*

⇒ *success*

In the New Testament, the Old Covenant blessings are extended to include:

...*every spiritual blessing in Christ.* Ephesians 1:3

As you know, the Old Testament physical blessings have never been revoked. Instead, they now come to you alongside all the spiritual blessings that the Holy Spirit pours into your life.

You can read about these blessings in Ephesians 1:4-14. They include:

⇒ *election*

⇒ *freedom*

⇒ *forgiveness*

⇒ *holiness*

⇒ *God's presence*

⇒ *adoption*

The Old Testament blessings came to Israel when they obeyed the Law of Moses. But the New Testament blessings are yours by grace through faith in Christ.

You receive them when you listen to Jesus and follow Him with living faith. They overflow to you, my friend, as you walk in step with the Spirit.

You're not called, however, to receive the blessings selfishly; you're called to pour them on to others. And you can do this by *announcing* blessings in the name of the Lord.

Bless those who persecute you; bless and do not curse. Romans 12:14

The Old Testament priests had a special calling to bless the people of Israel. God gave them an important blessing to announce which released God's goodness over the people.

This is the way you shall bless the children of Israel. Say to them:

'The Lord bless you and keep you; the Lord make His face shine upon you, and be gracious to you; the Lord lift up His countenance upon you, and give you peace.'

So they shall put My name on the children of Israel, and I will bless them. Numbers 6:23-27

God backed up every word of blessing that the priests pronounced. Now, as believers in Jesus, we're God's New Testament priests. He's given us His authority to bless others. We're called to announce His blessing in the name of Jesus!

What are curses?

When we bless someone, we announce God's well-being over their life. But God also judges sin, and He does this through curses.

God's first curses were pronounced in the Garden of Eden. His *curse on sin* brought the whole human race under condemnation. Even creation itself was subjected to futility. As a result, we still live in a fallen world of suffering and heartache.

When God announced this curse, He also revealed His mercy and grace. He told the serpent:

I will put enmity between you and the woman, and between your seed and her Seed; He shall bruise your head, and you shall bruise His heel.
Genesis 3:15

This was humanity's first promise of freedom from the curse on sin. God said that 'the Seed' of the woman would crush the serpent's head.

God was pointing to Jesus' victory on the cross – when He removed our sin, defeated Satan, and paid the price for the curse to be lifted! As believers on earth, we begin to experience the freedom of the cross. And when we reach heaven, we'll find that the curse on sin has been totally lifted.

BLESSINGS AND CURSES

> *God will wipe away every tear from their eyes; there shall be no more death, nor sorrow, nor crying. There shall be no more pain, for the former things have passed away.* Revelation 21:4

This shows you, my friend, how Satan operates. He works through sin and within the curse on sin. This is his only territory! He's a defeated enemy under the judgement of God. Once sin has been dealt with, Satan's power is completely broken.

He can influence only those who are under God's curse. Where there's no curse, the devil has no power. And Jesus defeated Satan on the cross by dealing with the curse on sin.

The curse of the Law

God gave the Law to the people of Israel. It kept them apart from other nations, and taught them the holiness of God. Their obedience to the Law released God's blessing, and their disobedience attracted God's judgement – or curses. You can read about this in Deuteronomy chapters 28 and 29.

Jesus has also dealt with *the curse of the Law*. When He died on the cross, He was made a curse. He took the curse of the Law onto Himself and opened the way for the blessing of God to come to people by faith in Himself.

Christ has redeemed us from the curse of the Law, having become a curse for us (for it is written, 'Cursed is everyone who hangs on a tree') the blessing of Abraham might come upon the Gentiles in Christ Jesus, that we might receive the promise of the Spirit through faith.   Galatians 3:13-14

This means that the curse of the Law has been lifted from all those who believe in Jesus. Life in the Spirit is a curse-free existence!

The good news, dear friend, is that you can learn to live in this freedom and to be released from every negative curse-pronouncement which has ever been made over your life.

The power of a curse

Because of this freedom in Christ, many people maintain that no curse can influence a Christian.

It's true that we've been set free by the blood of Jesus from every negative influence – including curses. But we have to be prepared to fight and stand fast in our freedom for it to benefit our lives.

Curses today

A curse exists when a supernatural dimension is added to the natural harmful power of the tongue.

We know that gossip, slander and negative speaking do great harm. Words can hurt more, and do much more damage, than 'sticks and stones'.

When someone speaks with the *intention* of hurting a person, family or situation, their words possess a certain natural power.

They probably don't realise, however, that their hurtful words can also be a 'prayer' which the evil one may choose to enforce. By saying, 'I wish you were dead', they may mean only to hurt the person emotionally; but the destroyer can take their request literally – and start to act upon it physically.

The devil delights to destroy and defame people, and curses can arouse his negative influences. The Bible teaches that those who utter a curse are ready to arouse demonic influence.

May those curse it who curse the day, those who are ready to arouse Leviathan. Job 3:8

Leviathan was a sea monster which is sometimes used in the Bible as a picture of Satan.

This verse shows that the devil can be roused into action when one person curses another.

Every negative word or curse-like pronouncement provides Satan with an opportunity to defame and destroy someone. Any word that you speak against yourself, or against others, exposes you and them to the destructive power of the enemy.

This is why it's so important that we learn to control our tongues.

The tongue defiles the whole body, and sets on fire the course of nature; and it is set on fire by hell...

No man can tame the tongue. It is an unruly evil, full of deadly poison...

Out of the same mouth proceed blessing and cursing. My brethren, these things ought not to be so.   James 3:5-10

All curses operate until they're revoked by the curser, or the victim is released the power of Jesus.

What causes a curse?

We've seen that curses arise when people use the enemy's weapons – hatred, negative speaking, a desire to harm. We must also remember, however, that the enemy cannot work through a curse unless there's *a good reason* for the curse.

Because of Christ's perfect obedience, God does not curse you, my friend, whenever you sin and disobey Him. But this doesn't mean that God will not lovingly chasten you when you persist in sin.

For this reason, many are weak and sick among you, and many sleep. For if we would judge ourselves, we would not be judged. But when we are judged, we are chastened by the Lord, that we may not be condemned. 1 Corinthians 11:27-32

The Bible describes those sins which prompted God to curse Israel. Although He does not curse us automatically every time we sin, we'll obviously want to please Him by avoiding these sins.

⇒ *anti-Semitism* – Genesis 12:1-3

⇒ *worship of false gods* – Deuteronomy 27:15

⇒ *disobedience to God* – Deuteronomy 27:26

⇒ *misusing God's name* – Jeremiah 29:23

⇒ *dishonouring parents* – Exodus 21:17

⇒ *sexual sin* – Leviticus 20:10-16

⇒ *occult activity* – Leviticus 20:27

Freedom from curses

All curses were destroyed at the cross. They lost their power over you when you came in repentance and faith to Christ. You've been released, my friend, in Jesus' powerful name! Hallelujah!

When the chastening hand of God touches your life, you can repent and quickly find freedom. God will renew you, and restore you to Himself.

Some curses, however, are enforced by demons: and we need the Spirit's discernment to recognise them. It doesn't honour God when believers start delving unnecessarily into their pasts for evil influences. God has set you free in Christ, and this freedom is complete.

But the Spirit may show you that there's something in your life which is the result of a demonically-enforced curse. If this is so, you'll need to stand in your freedom in Christ, and enforce this against the activity of the enemy.

Demonically enforced curses

There are several evidences which point to the existence of demonically-enforced curses. These normally operate in *several members* of a family or a group, and are often found over *several generations*.

They're *persistent problems* which defy medical analysis or treatment. And they seem to take on supernatural characteristics – they're not just natural events or a series of coincidences.

There's normally a persistent history of *several evidences*. There'll be a whole pattern of events, not an isolated occurrence.

Experience suggests that the following matters can point to the existence of a demonically-enforced curse:

⇒ *repeated suicide attempts in many generations*

⇒ *repeated miscarriages, or unusual difficulties at menstruation or menopause*

⇒ *repeated acute sickness, mental and physical, with no clear medical diagnosis*

⇒ *a highly improbable rate of accidents*

⇒ *repeated marriage breakdowns, alienation, unforgiveness and family strife*

⇒ *continual and unnatural levels of debt and inability to make ends meet, particularly when there's no adequate explanation for this*

Dear friend, please don't go looking for these things in a negative or morbid way. You must submit yourself completely to the leading of the Spirit, and then check your thoughts with a wise and experienced leader.

It's best to wait until there are several evidences before even considering the possibility of a demonically-enforced curse.

If you really do suspect a curse, make sure that you check the answers to your questions very carefully. Verify *facts* wherever possible. Don't jump to conclusions. And *never doubt the power of the Holy Spirit to set people free!*

Remember, the victory was won at the cross – we're merely enforcing it.

In the next chapter, you'll learn how you can be released from *any* evil curse which is influencing your life, and how you can minister God's release to others – especially to the members of your own household.

12

Freedom from curses

Great damage can result from assuming that a person is cursed. Too many believers tell someone that their problem is a curse without investigating the situation carefully.

Dear friend, never suggest that a person is cursed without the Spirit's clear insight that a demonic curse is operating in their life. You simply must receive the spiritual gift of *discerning spirits* before making any pronouncement in this area.

At the same time, you must never forget that curses really do exist. And they're likely to become more common when churches confront the forces of darkness with a stronger Christian witness.

Countering a curse

The Scriptures make it abundantly clear that we should counter a curse with God's blessing.

Bless those who curse you, and pray for those who spitefully use you. Luke 6:28

Do not be overcome by evil, but overcome evil with good. Romans 12:21

Being reviled, we bless 1 Corinthians 4:12

This means that, if you're cursed in the course of your life, you should pronounce God's well-being over the person who opposes you. You should want God's best for that person – not the devil's worst!

It also means that, before we seek to release a cursed person or family, we must help them to move from the place where the curse is effective to the place where they can receive God's blessing.

The cross of Christ is the only basis for this exchange. *Unless people are in Christ, they cannot be released from a curse.* By faith, they must themselves claim the benefits of Jesus' blood.

Remember, dear friend, the ministry of release can be truly effective only when the person is in vital fellowship with *Christ* and a local church.

The ministry of release

The following suggestions are simply *guidelines* for the release of a person, a family or a group, from a demon-enforced curse. You must have the Spirit's guidance at every point in the ministry process.

⇒ Make sure that there's real personal repentance. This may involve representative *confession* for the sins of other people in the family or group. But remember, you can't *repent* for another person's sins. Everyone must repent personally.

⇒ Ensure that genuine confession of faith in Christ follows repentance. The person you're seeking to help must trust Christ's work on the cross for their release from the curse and their transfer to blessing. There can be no religious or folklore substitute. True freedom is found only in Jesus.

⇒ Establish a clear scriptural basis for release. The person must understand that God's blessing flows from His Word. Galatians 3:13-14 is a good Scripture to use. In *God's Word in My Mouth*, I suggest many powerful scriptures which you can use in a wide range of situations.

⇒ Make sure that the person renounces and revokes any contact with evil – either in them or in their immediate friends and family.

⇒ Ensure that forgiveness is extended wherever it is needed, and that all bitterness is renounced. This should be extended to the person who spoke the curse and to the one who's sin allowed the curse to take effect.

⇒ Announce release in the name of Jesus, under the anointing and authority of the Holy Spirit. When possible, a person in spiritual authority over the person – the husband, father or a leader from their church – should do this.

⇒ Forbid the demon that's enforcing the curse from bringing any further suffering to the person, and to their family and descendants. Announce this in Jesus' name.

The demon should be told that the blood of Jesus is the person's perfect protection, and that the blessing of the Lord is now replacing the influence of the curse.

⇒ Lay hands on the person and announce God's blessing. If they've not been filled with the Spirit, pray for this important blessing.

The person or people concerned must begin to walk in the blessing of God following the time of ministry. This means that you must help them to take up their personal responsibility in the Word and in personal prayer. Encourage them to live in obedience to God and to maintain close fellowship with the Lord and His people.

Spiritual release is always immediate; it doesn't depend on what anyone feels! It does, however, take time to learn to walk in Christ's freedom.

As with all aspects of release from demonic influence, it's important to remember this spiritual principle: *deliverance plus discipline equals true freedom!*

A prayer of release

Pause now, and think about the negative words which may be affecting your life. Ponder on this prayer declaration, and then speak it boldly to God.

"Father God, in the all-powerful name of Jesus Christ, I take authority over every negative word which has ever been spoken against me.

"I cancel and nullify them now.

"By the blood of Jesus, I am released from every evil influence, and from every curse, which has been made against me.

"I return blessing for cursing, and declare that I am blessed with every blessing in Christ. Amen."

13

Freedom for your family

By now, my friend, I'm sure you know that God has many covenant promises for you and your family. Jesus has purchased them with His blood, and He's waiting for you to lay hold of them.

Many believers, though, find this difficult. Their victory is complete. Their position before God is secure. Yet, so often, there seems to be a blockage.

Barriers to blessing

Many things can block the blessing that Jesus has made available. You can read about some of them in the other books in this LIVING WORD SERIES.

In *Prayer that Gets Answers*, for example, you'll learn how to overcome fear, failure, unbelief and the other things which block your prayers.

And in *God's Word in my Mouth*, you'll find many powerful faith declarations which can remove the mountains that block the blessings of God.

There are some barriers, however, which seem especially to block the blessings overflowing to us as *families*.

Consider this New Testament passage.

You were not redeemed with corruptible things, like silver or gold, from your aimless conduct received by tradition from your fathers, but with the precious blood of Christ, as of a lamb without blemish and without spot.   1 Peter 1:18-19

Look carefully at the phrase, 'your aimless conduct received by tradition from your fathers'. It refers to something which is handed down to us from past generations – to things which affect how we live and what we experience today.

The New International Version translates this as, *'You were redeemed from the empty way of life handed down to you from your forefathers'*.

Problems from past generations

We all carry some sort of baggage from the former generations of our families which produces an 'empty way of life' – a life *outside* God's blessing.

This is the way of life from which we need to be redeemed – to be set free.

This is exactly what Jesus has done for us through the blood of His cross. He has redeemed us from every inherited pattern of emptiness. The blood has taken care of it!

Why, then, do so many Christians still live empty lives without much evidence of God's rich blessing? The answer, dear friend, is that it's one thing to quote a good verse, but quite another thing to live in the good of the verse!

As with every divine promise, it may be necessary to take God's Word and to grasp it *aggressively*.

You may have to fight for your rights in Christ, and enforce them against the wishes of the enemy – like the people of Israel in the promised land.

Of course, you don't have to fight God! He's *already* provided complete freedom for you and your family. No, the problem lies elsewhere.

Natural attachments

First, there's your own attitude to these things. It stands to reason that generational problems run very deep. We tend to be very attached to the things we inherit – attitudes as well as antiques!

Family traditions die hard. Attitudes and beliefs which we picked up from our parents (which they learnt from their parents) can be firmly embedded in us. We may not even be aware of them.

Supernatural dimension

Then there's a powerful spiritual dimension to generational problems. If God loves to bless the family blood line, you can be sure that the devil wants to curse it.

Curses and other forms of spiritual bondage often run in families. Remember, we're not islands in the sea of life. Our actions and attitudes affect others – especially our children. The sins of the parents really are visited upon the children.

The devil loves to get behind this 'family dynamic' and assert a family bondage through it.

One Sunday, during a ministry time, I was asked to pray for a young Chinese woman who'd been having a tough time spiritually. As I began to pray for her, I heard a cold and menacing voice say: 'You can't have her. She's mine. She was given to me at birth.'

I stopped ministering and asked the Lord what this meant.

Immediately, I saw in my mind's eye a baby before what seemed to be some sort of pagan altar. I saw incense burning and an offering being made. I recognised the ritual from my knowledge of world religions and asked the woman if her parents were Buddhists.

'No', she replied, 'My parents belong to no religion, and I'm a born-again Christian.'

I then asked whether she'd been dedicated at a temple when she was born. She was sure that she hadn't. But I persisted.

'What about other members of your family?' I asked, 'Your grandparents? Your Uncles and Aunts?' She acknowledged that her grandmother went to a Buddhist Temple regularly.

'And what about when you were born?' I asked.

'My grandmother would have gone to the Temple and burned incense on my behalf.'

My spiritual 'picture' was confirmed. It was plain that the Holy Spirit had highlighted a negative influence which was operating in this family. We prayed together, and she was completely set free.

But, up to that point, she'd had no idea of the baggage from her generational past.

Some people argue that it's impossible for these negative elements to affect us once we've been born again and cleansed by the blood of Jesus.

I agree. We *are* redeemed. We *have* been set free by the blood of Jesus from *all* these things. This is a spiritual reality and an accomplished fact! But this doesn't mean that we enjoy this freedom in our personal experience *automatically*.

Far from it! You're in a fight, dear friend. A battle's raging in your mind, your will and your emotions. You must stand firm and live according to your position. You must actively lay hold of your blessings and possessions in Christ.

Sometimes this is a simple matter of claiming the promise of the Word – and you experience God's freedom immediately! At other times, though, you must fight, and fight, and keep on fighting, before you experience the victory which is yours by right.

14

Can the devil curse you?

There are two great dangers which you must avoid when you're dealing with your enemy, the devil.

⇒ *never underestimate his power and influence*

⇒ *never exaggerate his role*

Don't ever think, dear friend, that the devil can't touch you; and please don't blame him for every head-cold and red traffic-light. He isn't nowhere; but equally, he isn't everywhere!

The devil is a formidable enemy. He's powerful, but he's also defeated! Some believers seem to feel the devil's influence everywhere. But I'd much rather be super-sensitive to Jesus' presence!

You can be sure, my friend, that you've nothing to fear from the devil when you're walking with Jesus Christ. Hallelujah!

The Balaam principle

The Old Testament book of Numbers describes the important story of Balaam and Balak in great detail. It's a story which reveals much about the spiritual principles of cursing and blessing.

Balak, the king of the Moabites, was worried because the people of Israel had camped on his borders. He knew that the Israelites were too strong for his army to defeat, so he sent for Balaam.

Balak wanted to pay Balaam to curse Israel so that the Moabites could defeat them in battle.

It's hard to know whether Balaam was a false prophet, a backslidden prophet, or a mixture of both. We do know, however, that he tried to curse the people of God, and that the Lord wouldn't allow him!

Three times, Balaam tried to curse Israel; and, four times, a blessing came out of his mouth!

Not unexpectedly, this infuriated king Balak.

What have you done to me? I took you to curse my enemies and look, you have blessed them beautifully! Numbers 23:11

Balaam, however, knew the spiritual principle that nobody can curse those whom God has blessed.

How shall I curse whom God has not cursed? And how shall I denounce whom the Lord has not denounced? Numbers 23:8

Can you see where Israel's protection come from? It was the Lord's blessing which kept them safe.

They were blessed by the unbreakable covenant of God. They were 'set apart', and God was with them. Under the Old Covenant, they were safe while they walked in obedience to the Lord.

You can see this in one of Balaam's oracles, where he reveals the reason for Israel's protection.

I have received a command to bless. He has blessed, and I cannot reverse it. Numbers 23:20

Balaam goes on to underline the condition that Israel needed to fulfil to stay in the blessing.

He has not observed iniquity in Jacob, Nor has he seen wickedness in Israel. The Lord his God is with him, and the shout of a King is among them.
                                          Numbers 23:21

It was this insight which gave Balaam the idea of how he could curse the people of God. He knew that he could curse them if they disobeyed God and moved away from the safety of His blessing.

Few people link what happened next to Balaam. Yet Numbers chapter 31 shows that it was orchestrated by this hireling prophet. Balaam counselled the Moabite women to seduce the Israelite men and trespass against the Lord.

The men of Israel began to commit harlotry with the women of Moab. This led them to start participating in pagan sacrifices and worshipping the Moabite god. (You can read about this in Numbers chapter 25.)

God's anger was aroused, and He judged His people with a plague which killed 24,000 men and women. God's judgement was lifted only after all those who'd committed idolatry had been killed.

Balaam knew that he could not curse the people of God, but that God's protection would be lifted if they sinned. He knew that God would allow some evil to oppress the people – and this is exactly what happened.

The Pergamos principle

The story of Balaam has a direct relevance to the New Testament Church.

In the book of Revelation, John records the messages of Jesus to seven churches in Asia Minor.

Jesus' message to the church in Pergamos focused on the way that they'd compromised.

I have a few things against you, because you have there those who hold the doctrine of Balaam, who taught Balak to put a stumbling block before the children of Israel, to eat things sacrificed to idols, and to commit sexual immorality. Revelation 2:14

A clear warning then comes,

Repent, or else I will come to you quickly and will fight against them with the sword of My mouth. Revelation 2:16

God still takes sin and disobedience very seriously. There can be no place, my friend, for compromise in your walk with the Lord. You're living dangerously when you disobey God deliberately. The Holy Spirit can lift His protection and expose you to the loving judgement of God.

Of course, this doesn't mean that you'll be at risk of eternal separation from God.

There is no condemnation to those who are in Christ Jesus. Romans 8:1

Instead, it means that you'll miss many of God's blessings – both on earth and in heaven – and that you may experience the Lord's gracious chastening, which He sends to restore us to Him.

We must all appear before the judgement seat of Christ, that each one may receive the things done in the body, according to what he has done, whether good or bad. 2 Corinthians 5:10

This is a salutary reminder. On the one hand, the devil cannot curse those whom God has blessed. On the other hand, though, the Lord Himself will chasten those whom He loves.

It's vitally important, my dear friend, that you keep on walking in obedience before the Lord. If you do sin, quickly confess it to Him and repent.

Remember, He is faithful and just to forgive your sin and cleanse you from all unrighteousness.

The basic principle

Never forget the basic principle. The devil's a defeated enemy. Neither he, nor any of his demons, can plant a curse where there's no just cause.

Like a flitting sparrow, like a flying swallow, so a curse without cause shall not alight. Proverbs 26:2

God's New Covenant promise still stands true. You're set free from every negative effect of the enemy in your life. The blood of Jesus has dealt with him and his works.

As you walk in obedience and cleansing with the Lord, so He'll turn every curse into a family blessing – just as He did with the people of Israel.

The Lord your God would not listen to Balaam, but the Lord your God turned the curse into a blessing for you, because the Lord your God loves you. Deuteronomy 23:5

15

Freedom from the past

The glorious good news of the gospel proclaims that you were set free from your past when you trusted Jesus as your personal Lord and Saviour.

Every single thing that you've thought, or said, or done, which is contrary to God's will, has been totally removed by His blood!

The blood of Jesus Christ His Son cleanses us from every sin. 1 John 1:7

You're free, my friend! You're clean! You're forgiven! – in Jesus' precious name. Your freedom is absolute and eternal. It's total and complete. You'll never see your sins again.

You're free from them forever! The devil might try to remind you about them, but God has removed them forever!

The sins of past generations

But what about the sins of your ancestors? Are you free from their effects?

If God visits the parents' sins upon their children to the third and fourth generation, what happens to these 'generational sins' when we trust in Jesus?

The good news is that He provides a full and complete salvation. Nothing is left out. This means that all our sins are removed – past, present and future! This is what it means to be 'justified'.

Therefore since we have been justified by faith, we have peace with God through our Lord Jesus Christ. Romans 5:1

'Justification' is a legal word which means that you've been declared 'not guilty' because Jesus has already been found 'guilty' of your sin – and punished accordingly.

God sees you now as perfect and sinless. Not because of your merit, of course, but by His grace through your faith. Not by your fleshly works of righteousness, but by the perfect blood of Jesus.

His blood is so powerful that it reaches even to the generations which have gone before. It sets us free from any inherited effects of the sins of our parents – even to the third and fourth generations.

This is included in what Peter means here:

You were redeemed from the empty way of life handed down to you from your forefathers...with the precious blood of Christ 1 Peter 1:18-19 (NIV)

There's only one force which can release us from our forefathers' negative influence. It's not the latest self-help book; it's not a psychological technique; it's the precious blood of Jesus. And the blood has done its powerful work. We're free!

If the Son makes you free, you shall be free indeed. John 8:36

One of my colleagues is the heir to an ancient Scottish title. Back in the early fourteenth century, one of his ancestors was executed for treason against the English king, Edward I, and his body was displayed on London Bridge.

HOUSEHOLD SALVATION

A few years later, this man's son betrayed the Scottish king, Robert the Bruce, just before the Battle of Bannockburn, and had to flee for his life.

Because of these treacherous acts, it seems that the men of the family were cursed – and the male line died out after four generations.

In the following 600 years, several attempts were made to re-instate the title. Each time, however, the male line died out around the fourth generation.

At the end of last century, the title was restored again. My colleague's father's family is now the third generation since that restoration.

The father's two brothers have no sons. His first wife died after having only daughters, and one of his second wife's two sons has also died.

This means that my colleague is the only chance for the male line to survive beyond the fourth generation!

Praise God, therefore, that the father became a believer. He served as a Christian minister for 50 years, and the son is a Spirit-filled pastor.

The blood has done its work. The curse – which manifested itself for almost 700 years in divorce and a cessation of ancestry – has been broken.

A great deliverance

Consider for a moment, dear friend, the sheer magnitude of your deliverance.

If the iniquity of the parents is visited upon the children to the fourth generation, we can be effected by the sins of *fourteen* people in our family tree. And this number is *doubled* when we marry!

Without the blood of Jesus, what hope would there be for our freedom?

Sin pollutes and destroys; it spreads its evil influence; it carries a curse and reaps a terrible harvest. All these negative effects pass down the generations – until Christ's blood wipes them out.

These negative influences come in many forms. They can be both physical *and* spiritual.

Hereditary sickness

Sickness can be passed down the generations. Even the medical profession now accepts that many diseases are hereditary.

Some illnesses may touch different generations simply because the parents' sins are being visited upon their children – without a recognised cause.

Inherited sin

There's also the possibility of inherited sin. The sins of the parents can be reproduced in their children. Again, this can be more than the natural outworking of genetics or upbringing. It can be the judgement of God.

All kinds of sinful bondages appear to be passed down the family bloodline. Alcoholism, sexual immorality, divorce, criminal activity – they all influence the generations to come.

Children learn about sin from their parents, and can unconsciously pick up their sinful habits.

This is how sin entered the human race. Adam's sin came upon all those who followed after him: his children inherited his sinful nature.

If our forefather Adam's sin still affects our lives today, don't you think it's likely that the sin of our more immediate parents affects us too?

Demonic influence

Demonic activity can also be passed down the generations. It seems that even the devil tries to work through the family bloodline. The book of Genesis speaks about the 'seed of the serpent'.

I will put enmity between you and the woman, and between your seed and her Seed. Genesis 3:15

Whatever else this means, it shows that evil influences can operate through the generations.

We see this in the nations who opposed Israel. The Amorites, Amalekites and Philistines, for example, were Israel's enemies for generations. And the 'seed' of Ishmael and Isaac have been hostile to each other for over 4,000 years.

We also see it in the descendants of Joab. After Abner had made peace with David, Joab took his personal revenge on Abner and murdered him. When David heard about this, he cursed Joab with a judgement which passed down the bloodline.

My kingdom and I are guiltless before the Lord for ever of the blood of Abner. Let it rest on the head of Joab and on all his father's house; and let there never fail to be in the house of Joab one who has a discharge or is a leper, who leans on a staff or falls by the sword, or who lacks bread.
2 Samuel 3:28-29

In this way, even demonic bondage can be passed down the bloodline. This can operate through curses and other negative influences which come under the category of God's judgement.

Perfect freedom

The good news, my friend, is that you've been set free from these things by the perfect blood of Jesus. When, by faith, you lay hold of everything that His blood has done, the result is perfect freedom.

This doesn't mean, of course, that there's nothing for you to battle against in these areas. In fact, you may have to take a *very* strong stand against hereditary influences from your past.

I've mentioned that my father was dedicated to God's work by my grandmother. Sadly, he didn't accept God's call, and died relatively young.

When I approached the age at which my father died, a strange fear come upon me. I resisted this fear, but it seemed to have an unnatural strength.

I felt that the enemy was trying to frighten me into believing that I'd die at the same age as my father.

When I recognised the fear's demonic origin, I fought it – in the name of Jesus. I took the New Covenant promises of God, and claimed my inheritance and freedom through Christ's blood.

This was something more than a psychological matter. It was a spiritual battle. I had to stand firm in my position in Christ. It was *not* an easy battle. But my freedom in Christ won through!

You may have to fight in a similar way to experience your freedom from the enemy's efforts to enslave you in some form of fear or bondage.

Remember your position. Know what Jesus has achieved for you on the cross.

Recognise that you really have been set free from the empty way of life handed down to you from your forefathers.

⇒ *You don't have to endure the same diseases as your parents.*

⇒ *You don't have to be afflicted by the bad temper that you inherited from your father.*

⇒ *You don't have to give in to the temptations which have ruined others in your family.*

⇒ *Your marriage doesn't have to end in divorce like your parents, or their parents before them.*

⇒ *You don't have to be affected by the demonic fears which have plagued your family for generations.*

You've been set free, my friend. So take your stand today against the wiles of the devil. Resist his every tactic and strategy.

Jesus is Lord over your spirit, so no other spirit can ever lord it over you! Hallelujah!

Pause again now, think about your freedom in Christ, then make this prayer declaration of deliverance to God.

"Father, I thank You that the blood of Jesus has set me free from the empty way of life which was handed down to me from my forefathers. I now stand in my freedom and liberty in Christ.

"I declare that I'm released from every curse and bondage of my bloodline.

"I'm cleansed from the iniquity of my forefathers.

"I'm set free from all forms of negative hereditary influence.

"I command my whole person to live in the good of this promise. And I declare that I'm sound in body, mind and spirit. My emotions and my will are fully subject to God's Holy Spirit.

"Jesus is Lord over my entire being. Praise His holy Name! Amen."

16

Honouring parents

Apart from marriage, your most important earthly relationship is with your parents. This is meant to provide you with a secure foundation for life.

God has ordained that children should be raised in a loving and stable family environment. This is why parents are called to raise their children in the nurture and discipline of the Lord. Children are 'on loan' from the Lord. It's a sacred trust.

Parents, therefore, should regard their children as a precious heritage and blessing from the Lord. And, as children, we should respect and obey our parents.

God commands us, dear friend, to honour our parents. This may seem difficult at times, because our parents often fall short of God's ideal. They make many mistakes.

But honouring our parents does not involve assessing their performance. We're called to honour them whether they've been good or poor parents.

You matter to God

You need to understand that your life is a gift from God. When you grasp this truth, you'll honour your parents as those who brought you into the world. They were God's vehicles of creation for you!

Were it not for your parents, you'd never have been born! This may seem too obvious to mention, but it's an important truth.

God says that your birth was not an accident. You were the deliberate act of God's creation. *He* formed you in your mother's womb. *He* created your inmost being – that mysterious inner part which makes you uniquely and wonderfully you!

God did this for a purpose. He made you to fulfil His divine plan. Your being alive matters to

God. You're significant to Him, and important for His purposes on earth. There's a special part of God's plan that *only you* can fill.

You're unique

You're one of a kind, my friend! Of course, like everyone else, you've been made in the general image of God; but, as a unique and individual act of creation, you carry God's image in a special way.

When people see you, they see the image of God uniquely reflected. Who you are – the person God made you to be – really matters!

Deep respect

Do you know how this wonderful creature came into being? Of course you do – it was through your parents!

This fact alone should fill you with gratitude and thanksgiving to God for your parents. And it should form the basis of a healthy respect for your mother and father.

This principle is so fundamental to our human well-being that God enshrined it in the Ten Commandments. In fact, it's the first commandment to come with a promise. Look how Paul refers to it.

First, he states the general principle of obedience to parents:

Children, obey your parents in the Lord, for this is right.   Ephesians 6:1

Then, he quotes the fourth commandment that God gave through Moses:

Honour your father and mother.   Ephesians 6:2

Finally, Paul points to the promise that God makes to all who obey this commandment.

...that it may be well with you and you may live long on the earth.   Ephesians 6:3

The power of the promise

God shows how important it is to honour our parents by making an outstanding promise to those who do. He says, 'Honour your *father* and your *mother* and it will go well with you. And you will live long on the earth!'

HONOURING PARENTS

Do you notice that Paul specifies both parents. You can't get away with honouring just your favourite parent, God wants you to honour both of them. After all, God used them *both* to bring you into the world!

I discovered the power of this promise many years ago when I was a young pastor. Day by day, I met people who came with their problems. As I listened carefully to them, I discovered a recurring theme.

They'd often say things like, 'I'm not sure what's wrong with me, it just seems as if nothing's going well.'

I must have heard this kind of statement hundreds of times! People of all ages came with many different problems. They had a variety of backgrounds; their experiences of life were dissimilar; yet they all had one thing in common.

Something seemed to be holding them back. They never seemed free to go forward. Success always eluded them.

Then, one day, I saw what was happening. The Holy Spirit opened my eyes to the real issue. It was God's command to honour our parents. In every situation that I'd been reviewing, the person had a problem with their attitude to their parents.

One young woman was having great difficulty breaking free from repeated acts of immorality. It was easy to see *where* she was going wrong. But *why* was it happening?

I discovered that she'd rebelled against her parents during high school. Her anger was particularly directed against her father because she felt ignored by him.

Her rebellion led her into an immoral relationship with an older married man. And she'd been trapped in a series of similar situations ever since.

Even when she repented of her physical actions, it seemed that a powerful force was holding her back.

I explained that her rebellion against her parents was the root of her problem. I showed her that, according to the Word of God, nothing would truly go well *until she repented of her dishonouring attitudes* and actions towards her father.

She repented for her inner attitudes, made her peace with her parents, and then was set gloriously free! Her life changed dramatically. She was released from her immoral life style and began to enjoy the blessing of God in all that she did.

For many people, the dishonouring of parents will not be so obvious. You may not consider yourself to be in open rebellion against your parents. But I've found that people often hold deep-seated feelings and attitudes which amount to much the same thing.

If you feel that your parents have ever let you down, (this probably includes all of us!) you must make sure that you're not harbouring any negative thoughts or judgmental feelings against them.

Refuse such things, dear friend, and ask God to release you from them. Remember, it's *extremely destructive to you and your well-being in life* to harbour any anger, bitterness or unforgiveness towards your parents.

No matter what wrong they committed against you – forgive them! Do it today. Do it now.

I suggest that you pray something like this:

"Dear Lord. I acknowledge You as my true God and my true Father in heaven.

"I thank You for Your perfection, for the gracious way that You deal with me, and for the tender way that You care for me.

"I confess to You now the anger that I hold deep within me against my mother and/or my father.

"They failed me. They were not there for me when I needed them. They said things and did things which hurt me. (Specify the details to the Lord).

"But I know that You have accepted me unconditionally, and that You hold me close to Yourself forever.

"I can forgive my mother and/or father because You have forgiven me. I release them from all the hurt they've ever caused me. I make it my choice, from this moment on, never to hold this against them again.

"I honour my mother and I honour my father. And I give You thanks for them both.

"Praise You Lord! Amen."

17

Parental blessing

The Bible teaches that our God is a God of absolute authority. He rules supreme. He's the Creator, the Most High, the only Lord in heaven and on earth: there's simply no other besides Him.

Because God has made humankind in His image, aspects of His authority run through humanity. We've been made, for example, to have dominion over every living thing; and every aspect of society is characterised by some sort of authority.

All human authority comes from God: it's given (or delegated) by Him for a purpose, and it's meant to be exercised under His rule and in His way.

Human positions of power or influence are not ends in themselves, my friend. They've been given so that we can serve and bless each other in the same manner that the Lord serves and blesses us.

Whoever desires to be great among you, let him be your servant. Whoever desires to be first among you, let him be your slave – just as the Son of Man did not come to be served but to serve and to give his life a ransom for many. Matthew 20:26-28

Family authority

God's fatherly authority is meant to be exercised in families through husbands and fathers. It's their holy function to accept full responsibility for the spiritual well-being of their whole family.

The husband is the head of the wife, as also Christ is head of the church. Ephesians 5:23

This means that the Father delegates His divine head-ship to human fathers and husbands. He expects them to care *spiritually* for their wives and children – and to do this in His serving way.

Husbands and fathers should accept their true position before the Father – as His delegated head of the family. When they neglect this spiritual responsibility, or it's usurped by the wife, the whole family is robbed of God's blessing.

This doesn't mean that men should act in an authoritarian way. Far from it! They are called to accept their spiritual responsibilities, but they're meant to exercise them in Christ's servant manner.

Too many men have tried to use the Scriptures to justify ordering their wives and children around.

Yet the Bible *never* instructs husbands to give orders to their wives. Instead, it keeps on commanding them to love their wives, and to love them in the same sacrificial way that Christ loved the church – that's genuine head-ship!

Husbands, love your wives, just as Christ also loved the church and gave himself for it.
Ephesians 5:25

This can seem rather hard for single mothers, and for men and women whose partners have left them. How can a husband love his wife when she's living with another man? And how can a family live under God's head-ship when the father is missing?

Although families are robbed of the physical blessings of companionship and finance when marriages collapse; they don't need to lose any spiritual blessings.

Husbands can go on loving their absent wives by speaking warmly of them, by praying for them, by acting well towards them, and by waiting for their restoration. Isn't this how Christ loves the church, which so often grows cold and leaves Him?

And God has given deserted wives and single mothers some special promises for their families:

You are the helper of the fatherless. Psalm 10:14

A father of the fatherless, a defender of widows, is God in His holy habitation. Psalm 68:5

The Lord relieves the fatherless and the widow.
Psalm 146:9

God promises single mothers that He, the ultimate Father, will act as the father in those families where the earthly father is absent. Isn't this wonderful!

This promise, which is repeated many times in the Bible, guarantees that no single mother need miss a single spiritual blessing.

Of course, this doesn't excuse churches from their responsibilities to support single-parent families. As the body of Christ, local congregations should care for broken families *practically* and cover them *spiritually* with the compassion and love of Jesus.

Parental authority

Within families, God has not only delegated *the Father's spiritual head-ship* to human husbands and fathers, He's also delegated His more *general trinitarian authority* to both earthly parents.

God has instituted parenting for the godly nurture and blessing of children. Parents are meant to care for their children in much the same way that the Godhead cares together for the whole creation.

Ideally, parents work together *co-dependantly* in the same way as the Father, the Son and the Spirit work together – with different functions and distinctive commitment.

Parents are God's representatives to their children. And He wants Christian parents to establish their homes according to His biblical standards of sacrificial love and merciful discipline.

Children growing in this sinful world need to be taught God's boundaries from the beginning. And God has appointed *both* parents to do this.

God's holy command to all children is this:

Children, obey your parents in all things, for this is well pleasing to the Lord.   Colossians 3:20

The parents' delegated authority couldn't be clearer. Children are to obey them 'in all things'. This means, of course, that parents have a greater responsibility. They must be good examples and representatives of God's nature and standards.

God's word to fathers takes this even further.

Fathers do not provoke your children, lest they become discouraged.   Colossians 3:21

It's clear that parental authority can be abused – and this is a serious offence before the Lord. One of the worst things that a parent can do is discourage a child through bad parenting.

Common mistakes

This happens through one of two mistakes.

Parents either under-discipline their children; they rarely correct them, or correct them inconsistently. Or they *over-discipline* them, and treat them harshly and repressively.

Neither way is right. Instead, God wants all His children to be brought up in the loving training and admonition of the Lord.

The best way to bless your children, my friend, is by giving them the parental nurture and discipline they need. Sadly, many parents go wrong.

When you discourage and wound your children, you can create resentment and dangerous attitudes. Your only solution is to confess your failure to the Lord *and to your children.*

Ask them for their forgiveness, and then begin again God's way. Let your children see their need to forgive you for your sin against them. This will release the blessing of God's healing and freedom into your family.

Harsh words damage lives

Children can be damaged for life when their parents abuse their authority.

For example, harsh words which are spoken rashly by a father or a mother can function like a curse over the child. How often, my friend, have you heard parents speak negative, destructive words over their children?

Often it's such things as, 'You're useless! You'll never amount to anything good!' Or, 'You're stupid! Why can't you do better at school.' It's impossible to exaggerate the damage that such words cause children.

It's not just the words themselves but the power and authority which lie behind them. Remember, such words can arouse Leviathan, and he delights to make the hurtful parental statement come true.

My dear friend, if you've ever been guilty of saying harsh and negative words in your 'parental office', repent now before the Lord. Revoke the words. Verbally cancel them out. Ask God to break their power. And seek your children's forgiveness.

God's words bless lives

There is, however, a positive dimension to this. God gives parents their authority in order to bless their children. And God has ordained parental blessing for the prosperity and spiritual well-being of children. It's time now, my friend, for you to learn how to pass on this blessing.

The Old Testament patriarchs knew the rightness and power of parental blessing. When

PARENTAL BLESSING

Isaac's time on earth drew to a close, he wanted to pass on his blessing to his first-born son, Esau.

When he realised that he'd been tricked into blessing Jacob, Isaac was distraught. He knew that the blessing had been activated and could not be revoked! That's the power of parental blessing.

When Jacob's blessed his children, he spoke a clear word over each son. He had a special blessing for his youngest (who normally inherited least) and for his grandsons who'd been born in Egypt.

You can read these powerful blessings in Genesis chapters 48 & 49. They're full of prophetic content. And, of course, God honoured Jacob's parental blessings: they all came to pass.

As a believer, God has given you the same parental authority. Wait on God for His prophetic word for your children. Ask Him for wisdom. Don't try to manipulate these things. It's the Word of the Lord that you want – God's will, not yours.

A special blessing

Your children are a special trust from the Lord and you're accountable to Him for their welfare in body, mind *and* spirit.

The Bible calls you to raise your children to go the way that *the Lord* has for them – not the way that you want them to go! That's what this well-known verse means.

Train up a child in the way he should go, and when he is old he will not depart from it. Proverbs 22:6

The three-fold priestly blessing from the book of Numbers is the greatest blessing that God has given you to use.

The Lord bless you and keep you;

The Lord make His face shine upon you, and be gracious to you;

The Lord lift up His countenance upon you, and give you peace. Numbers 6:24-26

As a New Testament believer, my friend, you're a priest. And, as a parent, you're called to function as a priest in your own home.

Priests were called to represent the people before God in intercession, to make sacrifices, and to *pronounce blessings* in the name of Israel's God.

This is your calling as a parent. Pray for your children. Pour your life into them sacrificially.

Speak God's Word over their lives. And bless them regularly with the words that God gives.

Israel's priests also had a governmental and educational role among the people of God. In the same way, Christian priestly parents are also called by God to do these things in their homes.

A well-ordered household, which prays together and learns the Word of God together, is a household where God's abundant blessings will be experienced and enjoyed – and will begin to overflow to others.

Pause now to think about your children, and the way that you treat them. Ask God to show you what action you need to take. Then make this prayer declaration to God.

"Heavenly Father, I take my place as the earthly father/mother of my child(ren).

"In the name of Jesus, I revoke any negative words that I've spoken, and all the negative attitudes I've held against my child(ren).

"I now pronounce the blessing of God over .... (name them all).

"I announce Your blessings of goodness, joy and peace to them, in Jesus' precious name. Amen."

18

The family altar

Throughout this book, dear friend, I've been showing you how much God wants to bless your family. Everything you've read should have underlined God's unbreakable covenant purposes for your household.

He promises you salvation, healing, provision, protection – and much, much more. By now, you should be 100% certain of the high priority that God places on His covenant relationship with the families of Christian believers.

In this final chapter, we'll draw everything together at the *family altar*. This is an expression which many people use to refer to the spiritual life and family worship of Christian households.

The church in your house

You're probably familiar with the New Testament verses which refer to 'household churches'.

In Romans chapter 16, for example, Paul greets his ministry companions, Priscilla and Aquila, and 'the church that is in their house'.

There were many similar churches in the larger households across the Roman Empire. They were properly constituted churches, not home-groups.

The extended family who lived in the home – including the slaves, servants, and others who lived there – formed the basis of each household church.

This shows that family homes were the heart of early church life. As the first Christians worshipped God in their homes, and reached out to other people around their homes, so the church grew.

This underlines how vital it is for you to have a strong, healthy, Spirit-filled family life. And this simply isn't possible without your family sharing together in worship, prayer and Bible reading.

In the book of Job, we read how Job acted as a priest in his home offering sacrifices for his family.

So it was, when the days of feasting had run their course, that Job would send and sanctify them, and he would rise early in the morning and offer burnt offerings according to the number of them all.
Job 1:5

And the second book of Samuel describes King David's spiritual actions at home.

The king was at the centre of the celebrations when the ark of the covenant came to Jerusalem. He led the nation in worship by blessing the people and offering sacrifices to God. But he didn't forget to return home to minister to his own household!

David returned to bless his household.
2 Samuel 6:20

Many people are active in God's work blessing others, but it's vital that they maintain a spiritual life at home in their families too.

Your family members, my dear friend, need you to be more committed to their spiritual well-being than to the well-being of others.

Infant baptism

The family altar begins at birth. Many branches of the church teach that the children of Christian parents should be baptised because of their place within the New Covenant.

I've carefully examined all the arguments for baptising the children of believers, and I'm not convinced that this is what the Bible teaches.

In the New Testament, every example of water baptism *follows* faith. As a sign and seal of faith in Christ, baptism can never come *before* we believe for ourselves.

He who believes and is baptised will be saved.
Mark 16:16

This doesn't mean that the children of Christian parents are outside the covenant, and should be treated as though they're no different from pagans.

Although I think that we should reject the practice of infant baptism, we have much to learn from the covenant teaching which lies behind it.

As we've seen, children are brought into the covenant blessings, and are sanctified, by the faith of believing parents. The faith and baptism of one parent is all that's necessary.

The moment that our children are old enough, they're responsible for affirming their place in the covenant by trusting Christ for themselves. And, in due course, they should be baptised in water when they know that they've made a life-long commitment.

But, until they're old enough, they should be treated as they are – as children of the covenant. This has real implications for work with children and young people, and for communion services.

Infant dedication

Does the rejection of infant baptism mean that there's nothing we can do for our children in presenting them to the Lord?

Of course not! It's natural for Christian parents to want to dedicate their children to God and to seek His blessing on their lives. So we should encourage them to come before their local congregation and thank God publicly for the birth of their children.

Some people criticise this practice as lacking scriptural foundation, but it seems to have more biblical support than infant baptism. After all, Jesus was dedicated as an infant and baptised as an adult – and that's surely a good example to follow!

When Jesus ministered on earth, many parents brought their children to Him to be blessed. Jesus' disciples, like many today, opposed this – but Jesus over-ruled them!

Little children were brought to Him that He might put His hands on them and pray, but the disciples rebuked them. But Jesus said, 'Let the little children come to Me, and do not forbid them; for of such is the kingdom of heaven.' And He laid His hands on them. Matthew 19:13-15

My own story convinces me that God honours the dedication of infants by Christian parents. As you know, my grandmother dedicated my father to the work of the Lord when he was in danger of death as a young boy.

God honoured that prayer, and its effects were felt in the next generation. Both my elder brother and I have experienced its power!

Baby dedication should not be just a traditional ritual in churches which reject infant baptism. It should be something special and prophetic – a meaningful commitment by the parents.

A middle-aged couple visited their pastor. They wanted him to speak to their son and persuade him not to take up a dangerous missionary post overseas. He was their only son and had just qualified as a medical doctor.

During the interview, the pastor recalled the day when their son had been dedicated to the Lord.

'It's seems only yesterday when you brought him before the Lord and dedicated him totally to the Lord for His use,' he said.

There was a tense silence. Then the parents smiled, 'Point taken!' they said. 'We dedicated him to the Lord, and we really meant it.'

Family worship

In many modern Christian homes, the daily family prayers and Bible reading of their parents' generation have been rejected as 'too legalistic'. Yet these traditional devotional disciplines have been replaced with absolutely nothing!

Family worship seems to be almost non existent today. What a pity! The family that worships and prays together really does stay together; and, in these days of divorce, we need every drop of domestic glue that we can find.

Family worship need not be a dull duty (but even that's better than nothing). It can be exciting, rather than something else to feel guilty about.

Meal times are often the best time for a few minutes of family worship. This is easy with small children, but harder to maintain with teenagers. Of course, there must be some discipline in maintaining family meals. It's amazing how few Christian families eat together every day.

Television kills conversation. Learn to switch it off! The telephone need not be answered for ten minutes. Unplug it or use an answer-phone! Talk to each other. Then, maybe, sing a song to the Lord, read a Psalm or Bible story, and pray.

Don't try to be too formal or ambitious in your family devotions; but it is vital that you do develop a family habit of prayer. Simple, short times are easy to maintain, and can be very effective.

It's also important to spend a few moments together in God's Word. There are many simple Bible reading aids that you can purchase from good Christian book-shops: these will help with your family devotions.

Some families find it helpful to keep a prayer notebook. You can set up a column for prayer requests. People in the family can then write in their prayer requests, and then they can all pray together about them. Make sure that you leave a column free for God's answers!

The joy of seeing God answer the needs and concerns through the family's prayers is indescribable. This is a great boost to faith, and a testimony to your children that God is real.

Of course, you must be sensitive to those who aren't believers. Don't force the issue. But don't leave them out and make them feel inferior.

Each family must learn how to see Jesus as their Head. And this head-ship must be seen through loving actions and not just external acts of worship.

Family communion

Before Jesus returned to the Father, He instituted a special family meal – the 'holy communion', 'eucharist' or 'Lord's Supper'. This was based in

THE FAMILY ALTAR

the Jewish Passover meal, although Jesus invested it with new meaning.

The Passover was (and still is) a great family occasion for Jews. We've already seen that the Passover is packed with significance for *household salvation*. And the same is true for communion.

The church in Jerusalem met in each other's homes and broke bread daily. The Jewish custom of beginning a meal by breaking bread was a natural setting for believers to remember Jesus as He'd commanded.

We can do something similar today, for family meals are the best and most biblical setting to celebrate communion.

He took bread, gave thanks and broke it, and gave it to them, saying, 'This is My body which is given for you; do this in remembrance of Me.'
Luke 22:19

The remembrance aspect of communion, however, is not just for us. It's also for Him. He remembers us as we remember Him. The bread and wine are nothing but simple reminders; but to God they're memorials which He sees. And when God sees, He acts!

God doesn't need to be reminded of anything, my friend, because He never forgets – so what does it mean when the Bible says that God *remembers*?

Quite simply, it means that He acts to fulfil His covenant promises.

For example, the Scriptures state that God remembered His covenant when the children of Israel were groaning under the burden of their Egyptian taskmasters. The Bible reports:

God heard their groaning, and God remembered His covenant with Abraham, with Isaac, and with Jacob. And God looked upon the children of Israel, and God acknowledged them.

Exodus 2:24-25

The rest is history. God acted according to His covenant and rescued them!

Communion, dear friend, is a covenant meal. When Jesus sees your family take the bread and wine in faithful obedience, He remembers them. This means that He acts to fulfil the covenant that He's made with your household.

The communion can be a powerful time of healing and restoration – a time of miraculous provision for the whole family.

Household Salvation

You've just about reached the end of the book now, so it's time for you to decide what to do next.

What will happen when you put the book down? Will you forget what you've read? Discuss it with a friend? Hope that it might be true?

Or are you going to allow God to use it to bring changes to your life – and to your family? Books like this can be full of fine theory, yet end up practically useless: it depends on your response.

You know that God doesn't work automatically in our lives. Instead, He calls us into a relationship with Him, into a genuine holy *partnership*.

For His part, He speaks, He guides, He equips, He strengthens. He provides us with the possibility of faith and obedience, and gives us the capacity to respond and walk with Him.

For our part, we must use what He gives, act on His words – and depend on Him at all times. That's as true in our families as in every part of our lives.

This has been a book about the greatest discovery that you can make – *household salvation*. None of the great discoveries of the past can match its impact on the lives of your loved ones. As you close this book, household salvation should be your greatest longing for every member of your family.

But there has to be change, my friend, or you'll never move from reading about God's blessings to *experiencing* His abundant freedom and joy.

For this to happen, there must be:

⇒ *a change in your thinking*

⇒ *a change in your attitudes*

⇒ *a change in your actions*

God wants you to accept the truths of household salvation, to take them deep into your spirit, and to start acting on them. They're meant to transform the way you think *and* the way you live.

Bin your traditional understanding. Discard your old individualistic ideas. Throw away the idea that nothing will improve. Change the negative way you think, and *believe* God's promises for your family.

God wants you to allow him to revolutionise your attitude to your spouse, your parents, your children, your brothers and sisters, your entire family.

Stop cursing them in your mind, my friend, and start blessing them with your mouth. Stop worrying about them, and start praying for them. Stop complaining about them, and start thanking God for them. It's time to look at them through *His* eyes.

I know it's not easy – these spiritual battles never are. But remember, God has put us in families to reflect His family image, and He purposes us to enjoy His family life within our natural families.

And we do. Most of us really do experience our greatest joys within our family circle.

But the devil hates families. Because they're God's appointed place for overflowing blessing, Satan does everything he can to smash them.

As a result, most of us experience our greatest heartaches in our family relationships.

We live under attack, in the tension between God's plans and the devil's pain. But we can persevere, we can overcome, and we can enjoy the victory that Christ has won for us.

No matter how grim your family situation, my friend, no matter how isolated you feel, no matter how abused and empty you are – God is breathing His covenant promises to you for your family.

If you believe them now, if you act on them faithfully, you'll soon see His blessings beginning to overflow through your family.

**Other books in this
LIVING WORD SERIES include:**

- Prayer that gets answers
- God's Word in my mouth
- The unlimited power of the blood

**For a full catalogue of Colin Dye
ministry products, please contact:**

Dovewell Mail Order
PO Box 9161
London
W3 6GS
England

Tel: 0171 727 8684
Fax: 0171 727 8716
e mail: ken-temp@dircon.co.uk
web site: http/www.ken-temp.org.uk